Praise for *Let's Take the Long Way Home*

"A near-perfect memoir: beautiful, humble, intimate and filled with piercing insights."
—*Time* (Top 10 Nonfiction Books of 2010)

"A lovely gift to readers . . . You can shelve *Let's Take the Long Way Home,* Gail Caldwell's beautifully written book . . . , next to *The Year of Magical Thinking,* Joan Didion's searing memoir about losing her husband. . . . But that's assuming it makes it to your shelf: This is a book you'll want to share with your own 'necessary pillars of life,' as Caldwell refers to her nearest and dearest." —*The Washington Post* (Best Nonfiction of 2010)

"High-spirited and heartrending." —*People*

"Stunning . . . gorgeous . . . intense and moving . . . a book of such crystalline truth that it makes the heart ache."
—*The Boston Globe*

"Female friendship is the beating heart of this book. . . . Pure tenderness . . . runs through its pages."
—*The New York Times Book Review*

"With humor and sadness . . . Caldwell gracefully weaves a thread of stories that describe and ponder friendship and loss. . . . A heartbreaker of a memoir."
—*USA Today* (10 Books We Loved Reading, 2010)

"[A] beautiful book . . . Caldwell's writing is serene, wry and meditative. . . . The losing isn't the exceptional part of this story; everyone loses something, sooner or later. The wonder lies in finding it in the first place."
—Salon

"Acutely observed and beautifully written . . . What an astonishing friendship. What great women. What a stellar, unforgettable book." —The Huffington Post

"A beautiful, poignant testament to what we can mean to each other . . . Caldwell is calm, clear-eyed, and sharp; this book is more about the depth and devotion of adult female friendships than about loss." —*Elle*

"This elegiac memoir of the author's alliance with writer Caroline Knapp . . . is a testament to the art of female friendship—and its necessity." —*More*

"[A] moving tribute to [Caldwell's] best friend."
—*O: The Oprah Magazine* (Best Nonfiction 2010)

"[Their] relationship nurtured and inspired Caldwell and Knapp, and in reading about it, we feel enriched as well."   —*Chicago Tribune* (Editor's Choice)

"So lovely and, somehow, so precise in its wisdom . . . I feel lucky to have met this graceful, piercing book."
—KELLY CORRIGAN, author of *The Middle Place*

"There are as many shadings to our griefs as there are lost loves to grieve over. Friendship, as Gail Caldwell's memoir gracefully testifies, asks a special, liberating eloquence." —RICHARD FORD, author of *Independence Day*

"Revelatory, joyous and inspiring . . . Intensely moving, without a hint of sentimentality, *Let's Take the Long Way Home*—part memoir and part biography of a friendship—should be read and cherished." —*The Bark*

"[A] heart-stopping memoir . . . even-handed, honest and straightforward . . . Caldwell is a skillful writer, both plain and wise, and, despite the devastating story, never, ever maudlin. . . . This lovely, strong book will make you weep, in sorrow for what was lost, in joy for what they had."   —Minneapolis *Star Tribune*

"An exquisite testament to the bittersweet depths of love and loss. If you've ever had a soul mate, whether human or canine, this book was written for you. If you haven't, this honest and liberating memoir will help you find one."   —PATRICIA B. McCONNELL, author of *For the Love of a Dog*

"As much an elegy as a remembrance of shared joys . . . Grief and love are perfectly balanced in this moving tribute to a friend—and to the dog who witnessed her joys and sadness."   —*Richmond Times-Dispatch*

"Caldwell summons up an incisive emotional clarity [in] this gift of a book."   —*The Christian Science Monitor*

"Eloquent . . . a moving account of Caldwell's grief for her friend."   —Cleveland *Plain Dealer*

"Caldwell's graceful account ensures that Knapp will be remembered not just for her tragic death but for her vigorous, rich life."   —*Parade*

"Gail Caldwell knows a thing or two about good writing. . . . Sure to appeal to anyone who has ever experienced true friendship."   —The Daily Beast

"*Let's Take the Long Way Home* is like Caldwell's previous memoir, *A Strong West Wind,* in its gorgeous language and lack of spectacle. . . . [It] is marked by its generosity and warmth. And its precision, as well."
     —*The Boston Phoenix*

"Poignant and powerful . . . Caldwell writes with deep feeling, but without sentimentality, about [a] life-altering friendship."   —*Kirkus Reviews*

"Luminous . . . spare but wrenching . . . Readers will . . . find themselves moved by Caroline, and will almost certainly be moved to tears."   —*BookPage*

"A gripping mix of confession, elegy, and resolve . . . an adroitly distilled memoir of trust, affinity, and love."
—*Booklist*

"Caldwell . . . has managed to do the inexpressible in this quiet, fierce work: create a memorable offering of love to her best friend, Caroline Knapp. . . . Caldwell is unflinching in depicting her friend's last days, although her own grief nearly undid her; she writes of this desolating time with tremendously moving grace."
—*Publishers Weekly* (starred review)

"Gail Caldwell portrays the experience of having a best friend with an unsentimental and unflinching dissection, richly mining a connection between two women built on conversations, experiences, and dreams. *Let's Take the Long Way Home* is an intimate reflection on one of the great gifts life can offer—that of a best friend."
—LEE WOODRUFF, co-author of *In an Instant*

"Out of a great loss, Gail Caldwell has fashioned a great gift: an intimate memoir that somehow contains everything that really matters about life. Lucid, elegant, passionate, wise, and enormously moving—a book of rare and memorable beauty."
—JOAN WICKERSHAM, author of *The Suicide Index*

BY

GAIL CALDWELL

New Life, No Instructions

Let's Take the Long Way Home

A Strong West Wind

LET'S TAKE THE LONG WAY HOME

RANDOM HOUSE TRADE PAPERBACKS

NEW YORK

LET'S TAKE THE
LONG WAY HOME

...

A MEMOIR OF
FRIENDSHIP

Gail Caldwell

Copyright © 2010 by Gail Caldwell
Reading group guide copyright © 2011 by Random House, Inc.

All rights reserved.

Published in the United States by
Random House Trade Paperbacks,
an imprint of The Random House Publishing Group,
a division of Random House, Inc., New York.

RANDOM HOUSE TRADE PAPERBACKS and colophon
are trademarks of Random House, Inc.

RANDOM HOUSE READER'S CIRCLE & Design is a
registered trademark of Random House, Inc.

Originally published in hardcover
in the United States by Random House,
an imprint of The Random House Publishing Group,
a division of Random House, Inc., in 2010.

LIBRARY OF CONGRESS CATALOGING-IN-PUBLICATION DATA
Caldwell, Gail.
Let's take the long way home : a memoir of friendship /
Gail Caldwell.
p. cm.
ISBN 978-0-8129-7911-4
1. Knapp, Caroline, 1959–2002—Friends and associates.
2. Caldwell, Gail—Friends and associates.   3. Journalists—
United States—Biography.   4. Critics—United States—
Biography.   I. Title.
PN4874.K575C35 2010
070.92—dc22
[B]   2009029384

Printed in the United States of America

www.randomhousereaderscircle.com

8 9

Book design by Barbara M. Bachman

for Caroline

The golden moments in the stream of life rush past us,
and we see nothing but sand; the angels come to visit us,
and we only know them when they are gone.

—GEORGE ELIOT, *Scenes of Clerical Life*

LET'S TAKE THE LONG WAY HOME

IT'S AN OLD, OLD STORY: I HAD A FRIEND AND WE shared everything, and then she died and so we shared that, too.

The year after she was gone, when I thought I had passed through the madness of early grief, I was on the path at the Cambridge reservoir where Caroline and I had walked the dogs for years. It was a winter afternoon and the place was empty—there was a bend in the road, with no one ahead of or behind me, and I felt a desolation so great that for a moment my knees wouldn't work. "What am I supposed to do here?" I asked her aloud, by now accustomed to conversations with a dead best friend. "Am I just supposed to keep going?" My life had made so much sense alongside hers: For years we had played the easy, daily game of catch that intimate connection implies. One ball, two gloves, equal joy in the throw and the return. Now I was in the field without her: one glove, no game. Grief is what tells you who you are alone.

I.

I CAN STILL SEE HER STANDING ON THE SHORE, A
towel around her neck and a post-workout cigarette in
her hand—half Gidget and half splendid splinter, her
rower's arms in defiant contrast to the awful pink bathing
suit she'd found somewhere. It was the summer of 1997,
and Caroline and I had decided to swap sports: I would
give her swimming lessons and she would teach me how
to row. This arrangement explained why I was crouched
in my closest friend's needle-thin racing shell, twelve
inches across at its widest span, looking less like a rower
than a drunken spider. We were on New Hampshire's
Chocorua Lake, a pristine mile-long body of water near
the White Mountains, and the only other person there to
watch my exploits was our friend Tom, who was with us
on vacation.

"Excellent!" Caroline called out to me every time I
made the slightest maneuver, however feeble; I was
clinging to the oars with a white-knuckled grip. At

thirty-seven, Caroline had been rowing for more than a decade; I was nearly nine years older, a lifelong swimmer, and figured I still had the physical wherewithal to grasp the basics of a scull upon the water. But as much as I longed to imitate Caroline, whose stroke had the precision of a metronome, I hadn't realized that merely sitting in the boat would feel as unstable as balancing on a floating leaf. How had I let her talk me into this?

Novice scullers usually learn in a boat twice the width and weight of Caroline's Van Dusen; later, she confessed that she couldn't wait to see me flip. But poised there on water's edge, hollering instructions, she was all good cheer and steely enthusiasm. And she might as well have been timing my success, fleeting as it was, with a stopwatch. The oars my only leverage, I started listing toward the water and then froze at a precarious sixty-degree angle, held there more by paralysis than by any sense of balance. Tom was belly-laughing from the dock; the farther I tipped, the harder he laughed.

"I'm going in!" I cried.

"No, you're not," said Caroline, her face as deadpan as a coach's in a losing season. "No, you're not. Keep your hands together. Stay still—don't look at the water, look at your hands. Now look at me." The voice consoled and instructed long enough for me to straighten into position, and I managed five or six strokes across flat water before I went flying out of the boat and into the lake. By the time I came up, a few seconds later and ten yards out,

Caroline was laughing, and I had been given a glimpse of the rapture.

THE THREE OF US had gone to Chocorua for the month of August after Tom had placed an ad for a summer rental: "Three writers with dogs seek house near water and hiking trails." The result of his search was a ramshackle nineteenth-century farmhouse that we would return to for years. Surrounded by rolling meadows, the place had everything we could have wanted: cavernous rooms with old quilts and spinning wheels, a camp kitchen and massive stone fireplace, tall windows that looked out on the White Mountains. The lake was a few hundred yards away. Mornings and some evenings, Caroline and I would leave behind the dogs, watching from the front windows, and walk down to the water, where she rowed the length of the lake and I swam its perimeter. I was the otter and she was the dragonfly, and I'd stop every so often to watch her flight, back and forth for six certain miles. Sometimes she pulled over into the marshes so that she could scrutinize my flip turns in the water. We had been friends for a couple of years by then, and we had the competitive spirit that belongs to sisters, or adolescent girls—each of us wanted whatever prowess the other possessed.

The golden hues of the place and the easy days it offered—river walks and wildflowers and rhubarb pie—

were far loftier than what Caroline had anticipated: She considered most vacations forced marches out of town. I was only slightly more adventurous, wishing I could parachute into summer trips without having to fret about the dog or shop for forty pounds of produce. Both writers who lived alone, Caroline and I shared a general intractability at disrupting our routines: the daily walks in Cambridge, Massachusetts, the exercise regimens we shared or compared, the meals and phone calls and hours of solitary work that we referred to as "our little lives." "Paris is overrated," Caroline liked to claim, partly to make me laugh; when she met a friend of mine one evening who was familiar with her books, he asked if she spent a lot of time in New York. "Are you kidding?" she said. "I hardly even get to Somerville." Wedded to the sanctity of the familiar, we made ourselves leave town just to check the vacation off the list, then return to the joys and terrors of ordinary life.

I HAVE A PHOTOGRAPH from one of those summers at Chocorua, framing the backs of my dog and Caroline's, Clementine and Lucille, who are silhouetted in the window seat and looking outside. It is the classic dog photo, capturing vigilance and loyalty: two tails resting side by side, two animals glued to their post. What I didn't realize for years is that in the middle distance of the picture, through the window and out to the fields beyond, you can make out the smallest of figures—an outline of Caroline and me walking down the hill. We must have been on our way to the lake, and the dogs, by now familiar with our routine, had assumed their positions. Caroline's boyfriend, Morelli, a photographer, had seen the beauty of the shot and grabbed his camera.

I discovered this image the year after she died, and it has always seemed like a clue in a painting—a secret garden revealed only after it is gone. Chocorua itself has taken on an idyllic glow: I remember the night Caroline nearly beat Tom at arm wrestling; the mouse that sent me onto the dining room table while she howled with laughter; the Best Camper awards we instituted (and that she always won). I have glossed over the mosquitoes, the day Caroline got angry when I left her in a slower-moving kayak and rowed off into the fog alone. Like most memories tinged with the final chapter, mine carry a physical weight of sadness. What they never tell you about grief is that missing someone is the simple part.

THE TWO OF US ROWED, together and in tandem, for five years after that first summer. We both lived near the Charles River, a labyrinthine body of water that winds its way through Greater Boston for nine miles, from upper Newton through Cambridge and into Boston Harbor, with enough curves and consistently flat water to be a mecca for rowers. Because Caroline was small in stature and could body-press more than her own weight, I got to calling her Brutita, or "little brute." The boathouses we rowed out of were a couple of miles apart, and I could recognize Caroline's stroke from a hundred yards away—I'd be there waiting for her near the Eliot Bridge or the Weeks Footbridge by Harvard, ready to ply her with questions about form and speed and where to position one's thumbs. When she went out hours ahead of me, she fired off unpunctuated e-mails as soon as she got home: "hurry up the water is flat." We logged hundreds of miles, together and solo, from April to November; she endured my calls, in those first couple of summers, to discuss the mechanics of rowing: "I want to talk about thrust," I would say, with insane intensity, or, "Did you know the human head weighs *thirteen pounds*?" "Ummmm-hmmmm?" she'd answer, and soon I would hear a soft *click-click* in the background—evidence that she had begun a game of computer solitaire, her equivalent of a telephonic yawn. At the end of the day, when we walked the dogs, we compared hand and finger calluses (the battle scars of good rowing) the way teenage girls used to compare tans or charm bracelets; because she was and always would be the better rower, I accepted her continual smugness and vowed to get even in the pool. One year for Christmas I gave her a photograph from the 1940s of two women rowers in a double at Oxford, England. She hung it on a wall near her bed, above a framed banner that read ZEAL IS A USEFUL FIRE.

Both pictures hang in my bedroom now, next to the photograph of the dogs. Caroline died in early June of 2002, when she was forty-two, seven weeks after she was diagnosed with stage-four lung cancer. In the first few weeks in the hospital, when she was trying to write a will, she told me she wanted me to have her boat, the old Van Dusen in which I'd learned to row and that she had cared for over the years as though it were a beloved horse. I was sitting on her hospital bed when she said it, during one of those early death talks when you know what is coming and are trying to muscle your way through. So I told her I'd take the boat only if I could follow rowing tradition and have her name painted on the bow: It would be the *Caroline Knapp*. No way, she said, the same light in her eyes as the day she had taught me to row. You have to call it *Brutita*.

...

BEFORE ONE ENTERS THIS SPECTRUM OF SORROW, which changes even the color of trees, there is a blind and daringly wrong assumption that probably allows us to blunder through the days. There is a way one thinks that the show will never end—or that loss, when it comes, will be toward the end of the road, not in its middle. I was fifty-one when Caroline died, and by that point in life you should have gone to enough funerals to be able to quote the verses from Ecclesiastes by heart. But the day we found out that Caroline was ill—the day the doctors used those dreaded words "We can make her more comfortable"—I remember walking down the street, a bright April street glimmering with life, and saying aloud to myself, with a sort of shocked innocence, "You really thought you were going to get away with it, didn't you?"

By which I meant that I might somehow sidestep the cruelty of an intolerable loss, one rendered without the willful or natural exit signs of drug overdose, suicide, or old age. These I had encountered, and there had been the common theme of tragic agency (if only he'd taken the lithium; if only he hadn't tried to smuggle the cocaine) or rueful acceptance (she had a good long life). But no one I had loved—no one I counted among the necessary pillars of life—had died suddenly, too young, full of determination not to go. No one had gotten the bad lab report, lost the hair, been told to get her affairs in order. More important, not Caroline. Not the best friend, the kid sister, the one who had joked for years that she would bring me soup decades down the line, when I was too aged and frail to cook.

FROM THE BEGINNING there was something intangible and even spooky between us that could make strangers mistake us as sisters or lovers, and that sometimes had friends refer to us by each other's name: A year after Caroline's death, a mutual friend called out to me at Fresh Pond, the reservoir where we had walked, "Caroline!", then burst into tears at her mistake. The friendship must have announced its depth by its obvious affection, but also by our similarities, muted or apparent. That our life stories had wound their way toward each other on corresponding paths was part of the early connection. Finding Caroline was like placing a personal ad for an imaginary friend, then having her show up at your door funnier and better than you had conceived. Apart, we had each been frightened drunks and aspiring writers and dog lovers; together, we became a small corporation.

We had a lot of dreams, some of them silly, all part of the private code shared by people who plan to be around for the luxuries of time. One was the tatting center we thought we'd open in western Massachusetts, populated by Border collies and corgis, because we'd be too old to have dogs that were big or unruly. The Border collies would train the corgis, we declared, and the corgis would be what we fondly called the purse dogs. The tatting notion came about during one of our endless conversations about whether we were living our lives correctly—an ongoing dialogue that ranged from the serious (writing, solitude, loneliness) to the mundane (wasted time, the idiocies of urban life, trash TV). "Oh, don't worry," I'd said to Caroline one day when she asked if I thought she spent too much time with *Law & Order* reruns. "Just think—if we were living two hundred years ago, we'd be playing whist, or tatting, instead of watching television, and we'd be worrying about that." There was a long pause. "What *is* tatting?" she had asked shyly, as though the old lace-making craft were something of great importance, and so that too became part of the private lexicon—"tatting" was the code word for the time wasters we, and probably everyone else, engaged in.

These were the sort of rag-and-bone markers that came flying back to me, in a high wind of anguish, when she was dying: I remember trying to explain the tatting center to someone who knew us, then realizing how absurd it sounded, and breaking down. Of course no one would understand the tatting center; like most codes of intimacy, it resisted translation. Part of what made it funny was that it was ours alone.

ONE OF THE THINGS we loved about rowing was its near mystical beauty—the strokes cresting across the water, the shimmering quiet of the row itself. Days after her death, I dreamed that the two of us were standing together in a dark boathouse, its only light source a line of incandescent blue sculls that hung above us like a wash of constellations. In the dream I knew she was dead, and I reached out for her and said, "But you're coming back, right?" She smiled but shook her head; her face was a well of sadness.

2

EVERYTHING REALLY STARTED WITH THE DOGS.
I had met Caroline Knapp briefly in the early 1990s,
when she was a columnist for *The Boston Phoenix* and I
was the book review editor at *The Boston Globe*. A collection of her columns had just been published, and someone had introduced us at a literary gathering that I was
finding insufferable. "Caroline has a new book!" our
hostess said brightly, certain that we each had something
to offer the other. After the woman had left us, we ex-
changed half smiles and rolled our eyes. I'd liked that
about Caroline immediately—no self-marketer here. She
seemed to wear her reserve like silken armor: the French-
manicured hand holding a glass of white wine, the shy,
resonant voice. We passed a few polite words of mutual
regard, then moved apart to make the necessary rounds.

When I saw her again, a few years later, standing near
the duck pond at Fresh Pond Reservoir in Cambridge,
we had both downscaled in appearance. Each of us had

young dogs, and a dog trainer we knew had recently mentioned Caroline to me. "Do you know Caroline Knapp?" Kathy had said. "She has a puppy, too. You remind me of each other—you should try to get together."

I had mouthed some vague assent, though privately I didn't see the resemblance. The Caroline I remembered had been way too well put together to match my presentation in those days. I had a year-old, sixty-pound Samoyed, and I was walking around with grass in my hair and freeze-dried liver in my pocket. I spent most of my time reveling in the wild pleasures of dog-raising, not much caring how I looked. But the woman I ran into at the pond that late-summer afternoon was a far cry from my memory of Caroline's earlier refinement. She was still shy, to the point of my thinking she didn't remember me. The veil of classy attire had been traded for sneakers and a careless braid; hovering over Lucille, her shepherd mix who was the same age as Clementine, she seemed as passionately monothematic about her dog as I was about mine.

I also knew, for reasons that were personal as well as public, that the white wine Caroline had been holding that night years before had been her magic scepter and dagger both. Public because Caroline had revealed as much in her memoir *Drinking: A Love Story*. This was the summer after the book's publication, and she'd been on enough talk shows and feature pages to be a publisher's dream girl. And she "showed well," as they say in the trade: There was the long blond braid, the beautiful

voice, the restraint that suggested wells of darkness behind all that mannered poise. The general assumption is
that most writers want nothing more than the kind of
success Caroline's book had just enjoyed. I had a different perspective, from experience and intuition. If writers
possess a common temperament, it's that they tend to be
shy egomaniacs; publicity is the spotlight they suffer for
the recognition they crave.

The personal empathy came from my comparatively
cloistered past: I had stopped drinking twelve years earlier, in 1984. But whereas Caroline had gone mainstream
with her addiction, I was old school and deeply private
about my own struggles with alcohol. I believed the
"anonymous" part of AA was there as a protective shield,
and I had worn it as such for years.

We traded a tentative hello at the pond that day while
the dogs introduced themselves more boisterously. "Caroline, do you remember me?" I said, and she smiled and
said yes. I said, "God, you've been going through it
lately—are you all right?" She looked surprised, then relieved. She told me later that she had been walking
around that day exhausted, half undone by the exposure
she was getting, and that talking to me had been a
balm—I was more interested in her dog than her book
sales. So was she: We were like new moms in the park,
trading vital bits of information about our charges that
was enthralling only to us. I mentioned a two-thousand-
acre wooded reserve north of the city called Middlesex

Fells, where I was training my headstrong sled dog to run off-lead, and Caroline asked how to get there. Because the route was complicated, I explained it self-consciously, afraid that she was being polite and I was being long-winded. The place was half an hour away, tough to find even without traffic, and only someone devoted to training, as I was, would ever bother to find it.

A week later, at the Fells, I heard someone calling my name across Sheepfold Meadow, and I saw Caroline on the edge of the grounds, waving and smiling. I was surprised and pleased—she must have actually remembered my byzantine directions, then followed through. Paying attention, I would come to find out, was one of the things Caroline did. She called me a few days later to propose a walk together; when she couldn't reach me, she called again. An introvert with a Texan's affability, I was well intentioned but weak on follow-through; not without reason did an old friend refer to me as the gregarious hermit. I wanted the warmth of spontaneous connection and the freedom to be left alone. Caroline knocked politely on the front door of my inner space, waited, then knocked again. She was persistent, she seemed smart and warmhearted, and—to my delight—she was writing a book, she told me when we spoke, about people's emotional connections to dogs. She seemed like someone for whom I wouldn't mind breaking my monkish ways.

That book became *Pack of Two: The Intricate Bond Between People and Dogs,* published a couple of years later;

Caroline gave me the name of Grace, and recast Clementine as an Alaskan malamute named Oakley. Within weeks after our encounter at Sheepfold Meadow, we were planning outings every few days; the Fells became one of our regular destinations. We ran the dogs for hours in those woods outside of town, and in other woods, searching out gorgeous reserves of forests and fields all over eastern Massachusetts. We walked the beaches that autumn, and the fire trails in winter, carrying liver snaps for the dogs and graham crackers for the humans. We walked until all four of us were dumb with fatigue. The dogs would go charging through the switchbacks while Caroline and I walked and talked—over time so much and so deeply that we began referring to our afternoon-long treks as analytic walks.

"Let's take the long way home," she would say when we'd gotten to the car, and then we would wend our way through the day traffic of Somerville or Medford, in no hurry to separate. At the end of the drive, with Clementine snoring softly in the back seat, we would sit outside the house of whoever was being dropped off, and keep talking. Then we would go inside our respective houses and call each other on the phone.

"What about the ponds freezing?" I said one evening after a walk in early winter, when the dogs were still blasting out into the water, oblivious to anything but their own joy. "I'm worried about the ice being thin, and the dogs going out to chase birds, and falling through—

you know this happens to someone every winter. Some dog runs out onto the ice, and the owner goes after her, and the dog manages to get out and the human drowns. And you know we would both go after the dogs."

Caroline listened to me rant—I came to realize that her listening could be so intent, it almost had a sound—and sighed before she answered. "We're going to have to start walking with a rope and an ax, aren't we?" she said. She always knew how to talk me down from the tree.

I suppose every friendship has such indicators—the checks and balances of the relationship that make it stronger or more generous than either of you alone. For both of us, in different ways, the volume of the world had been turned up a notch. Whether this sensitivity functioned as a failing or an asset, I think we recognized it in each other from the start. Even on that first afternoon we spent together—a four-hour walk through late-summer woods—I remember being *moved* by Caroline: It was a different response from simple affection or camaraderie. She was so quiet, so careful, and yet so fully present, and I found it a weightless liberation to be with someone whose intensity seemed to match and sometimes surpass my own. Her hesitation was what tethered her sincerity: As much as Caroline revealed in her books, she was a deeply private person who moved into relationships with great deliberation. I had known enough writers in my life, including myself, to recognize this trait: What made it to the page was never the whole story, but rather the writer's version of the story—a narrative with its creator in full control.

I also thought that first day, more than once, that Caroline wished she were someplace else, because she kept checking her watch—she must have looked at it, she believed covertly, a half dozen times. I would learn to live with this little ritual, which had nothing to do with me. It was a marker for Caroline's anxiety, a way to anchor her place in the world no matter how open-ended her schedule. But that day I found it unnerving, and I finally asked her if she had to be somewhere. She was mortified, I think, and apologized, and we walked until dusk pushed us out of the woods. Monitoring the increments of time, particularly since she had stopped drinking, was Caroline's stopgap against the free fall of the days.

And one other repeated gesture would touch me that day in a way I couldn't have articulated at the time. Determined to keep up with Clementine, I had become a devoted dog walker; I also had had polio as a child and so walked with a slight limp and imbalance in the world. However much I compensated by toughing my way through, I was frailer on land than I liked to admit. When we went out in late September, the forest floor was covered with newly fallen acorns, and I kept slipping on them and fell more than once. I was used to my lifelong ungainliness and said so, making light of it; what I didn't say was that I was accustomed to awkward responses. When I explained the limp by saying I'd had polio, people tended to be either overly concerned or uncomfortable. Caroline, who never seemed to doubt my capabilities for a moment, was neither. After that first stumble, whenever I slipped she would put out an arm to brace me; holding on to her became as natural as reaching for a branch. If I was an ambler by nature and ability, Caroline was a sprinter—she was fast, she was agile, and she was often in a hurry, whether she meant to be or not. But once she ascertained my usual gait, she slowed her pace to mine and kept it there.

EXCEPT FOR THE FACT that we had both had sisters, our childhoods had little in common. Caroline had been born a twin, appearing a few minutes after her sister, Becca, and the two had stayed close throughout their lives. Because I'd had a good friend in Texas who was a twin, I recognized in Caroline the parallel traits that seemed born of this primal dyad—she had a capacity for intimacy that could sometimes seem private and absolute. My sister was two years older than I, and I'd grown up accustomed to being both bossed around and looked after. I was the daughter of fourth-generation Texans from struggling farming families; my parents had settled in the desolate Texas Panhandle, and my dad had been a master sergeant in the Second World War. Caroline had led what she called a sheltered existence within the milieu of intellectual Cambridge. Her father, who had died a few years before I met her, was an esteemed psychiatrist and psychoanalyst; Caroline had identified with him and adored him. She told me early in our friendship, with no small degree of amusement, that when she was a little girl of six or seven, he had sat on the end of her bed with a legal pad, pen at the ready, and asked her about her dreams. Her mother was an artist and an introvert, and she had died a year after Caroline's father. So she had lost both parents to cancer when she was in her early thirties, a double injury that had been cataclysmic for her; she stayed drunk for another year, then drove herself to rehab in 1994.

I knew much of this from her book and some of it from what she told me that first long afternoon in the woods; I also learned that day that she had just separated from her boyfriend of six years—a large-hearted man who went by his last name, Morelli. The break turned out to be temporary, and after Morelli and I became friends, Caroline and I often called him "the last good boyfriend in America." All of this piecemeal story—the narrative unfolding in the early friendship—belonged to a sinewy, solemn woman who seemed to me like the kind of person you'd pick to drive the tractor home in a hailstorm. She was tough, she was unassuming, and I suspect her stalwart reliability, which revealed itself to me in more than one crisis, came in part from practice: Having survived both anorexia and alcoholism, she had already walked through her version of worst fears.

———

I HAD JUST navigated my own crossroads. I was in my early forties, at an age when the view from the hill can be clear and poignant both. The imagined vistas have become realized paths, and I think you may live in the present during those years more than any time since childhood. I'd spent my thirties in a big-city newsroom where adrenaline and testosterone were as pervasive as deadlines, and I'd recently given up a stint as book review editor to go back to my ordinary job as book critic for *The Boston Globe.* This transition, as well as the recent shifts in technology, allowed me to work from home and hang around with the dog, who quickly learned that reading was my equivalent of chewing on a bone. I had long thought that the gods had handed me work tailor-made for my idiosyncrasies: I was too opinionated to be a straight news reporter, too gadabout to be an academic. I was dreamy, stubborn, and selectively fanatical; my idea of a productive day, as both a child and an adult, was reading for hours and staring out the window. It was my good fortune that I had found an occupation requiring just these talents; now, with Clementine, I could spend whole days in near silence, reading or writing or speaking in the simpler, heart-sure vernacular of human-to-dog.

The first several months that Caroline and I knew each other come back to me with the scent of winter: the crisp, distinctively East Coast aura of snow and city streets and radiator heat. I gave her fur-lined mittens in November on her birthday; a few weeks later, we both begged off other Thanksgiving plans, then cooked a roast chicken together after a day in the woods with the dogs. The weather got worse and colder and we adjusted our schedules accordingly: She taught me how to walk across frozen trails and sideways down steep hills, digging my feet into the terrain. I taught her the freestyle in an in-door pool, coaxing her to lay her face in the water to learn to regulate her breathing, while she stood there cursing me and shivering.

It seems to me now that Caroline was always cold. After the anorexia of her twenties, she had stayed on the thin side of normal, and she would show up for our walks swaddled in layers of fleece. As often as possible we headed for the woods or the reservoir, but sometimes in the evening, when the New England sun had disap-peared at an early hour, we would sneak into the Harvard athletic fields, near where I lived at the time, so that the dogs could have an open space to run. The fields backed onto a public housing project, separated by a high, dilap-idated chain-link fence. Getting onto the hallowed grounds was a two-person job: One of us lifted the fence where it had come loose over a ditch while the other rolled under it with the dogs, then held it up from the other side. Our trespass was illegal as well as rough—it was the kind of thing I had done all the time as a girl in Texas—and I was glad that Caroline was willing; for all of her exploits in the drinking world, she still possessed a good-girl quality that I had never been able to muster. We'd stand there in the frigid dark, the dogs illuminated against the night sky by Clementine's whiteness and the lights from the ball fields. It was like being encased in a cave of quiet and cold, and we stayed until we couldn't bear it any longer, telling each other stories—Caroline in her new Ugg boots, shivering and smoking, with me getting an illicit, still pleasant whiff of the smoke (I had quit four years earlier). Sometimes we'd sink onto the ground and lean against the old tattered fence, letting the dogs rummage in our pockets for biscuits before they went tearing out into the dark again. We used to laugh that people with common sense or without dogs were somewhere in a warm restaurant, or traveling, or otherwise living the sort of life that all of us think, from time to time, that we ought to be living or at least desiring. But there was nowhere else I wanted to be, beyond sitting there on the hard earth under a night sky, watching the dogs and talking.

THOSE FIELDS WERE also where we had our first misunderstanding, or confrontation, or whatever you call the seemingly trivial empathic failures that serve as a testing ground and gateway for intimacy. By the end of that winter, it was clear that we cared for each other and the routines we had so quickly established; less acknowledged was the crucial place we were carving out in each other's lives. For a few days I had been bearing a bruise in silence that had to do with our regard for each other as writers: something so core to me that it still gives me pause to remember my discomfort. As a reviewer for a big daily newspaper, I was the older and more seasoned writer; Caroline was the young turk at the alternative paper who'd enjoyed a rush of attention for her memoir. Because we had known of each other for a few years before we'd met, we had relied on that implicit assumption between writers of recognizing the other's achievement; in most relationships, this commonality of purpose would more than suffice. But Caroline had never said anything directly about what I did or what she thought about how well I did it, though she had given me a copy of her memoir and asked repeatedly if I had liked it.

Now I see this in a different light: I believe she ⁄ me as the one with more of the power and less of t⁄ needs or demands. That day in the field, I had⁄ insight. A long piece I'd written for the *Glo*⁄ been published, and I was exhausted. We ⁄ along and Caroline had muttered some ⁊ about how hard I'd been working, tho⁄ the essay itself. Finally I blurted out⁄ something difficult—I need to kn⁄ about my work."

She looked at me aghast. "Oh n⁄ turned into my mother. I assume⁄

but I never told you." She rushed to reassure me, and we talked for the rest of the walk about what a swampland this was: the world of envy and rivalry and self-doubt (between women, and writers, and women writers), about insecurity and power differentials. We found out that day, fairly quickly, how great and complex our fondness was for each other; I also had my first sense of something central about Caroline that would become a pillar of our friendship. When she was confronted with any emotional difficulty, however slight or major, her response was to approach rather than to flee. There she would stay until the matter was resolved, and the emotional aftermath was free of any hangover or recrimination. My instincts toward resolution were similar: I knew that silence and distance were far more pernicious than head-on engagement. This compatibility helped ensure that there was no unclaimed baggage between us in the years to come.

As relieved as I was that day by the conversation, I was unnerved by my own vulnerability. It was as though Caroline and I had crossed into a territory where everything mattered and that we were in it together. "Oh no," said, half laughing but with tears in my eyes. "What is she asked, concerned, and I said, "I *need* you."

3.

SHE WOULD SAY, I THINK, THAT THE NEED WAS GREATER on her end. She was at the beginning of what would become a two-year separation from Morelli, with whom she'd been involved for years and whom she would later marry; she had recently lost both parents; and she saw me, probably through an idealizing lens, as a competent woman who had built a life alone. The more complicated truth was that I was also at a pivotal point: I'd given up a lot of what didn't work, and drinking was only the beginning of the list. "You chose solitude," another friend had told me. "Well, I think solitude chose me," I said. "The old bride-of-Christ thing." Still, I'd always been comfortable in my own company, sometimes to the displeasure of friends or romantic partners. My last love interest of any importance had ended, badly, a few years earlier. One of my closest friends from the past decade, an artist and filmmaker, had just left Cambridge for New York. I had a number of old and solid friendships, male and female both, but these days most of the local ones belonged in the second circle of intimacy—the people you'd call when you were hit by a bus, but not necessarily if you'd merely sprained an ankle.

"Men don't really understand women's friendships, do they?" I once asked my friend Louise, a writer who lived in Minnesota. "Oh God, no," she said. "And we must never tell them." The fact was that I had been weaned on intense and valiant friendships among women, thanks to the milieu in which I'd come of age in Texas. I was in my early twenties during the heyday of the antiwar movement and the rise of feminism in the 1970s, which in Austin were closely linked. The women I knew there had burned the old rule book: the one in which women shopped instead of talked, competed for the silverback through any means, protected their fears and longings from one another as if they were professional trade secrets. I'd been part of an all-girl rock-'n'-roll band that got arrested together; we had relied on one another through whatever trials the decade presented, from medical school to drug addiction. When I left Austin for New England in 1981, intent on becoming a writer, what courage I possessed came in part from those passionate connections.

The women I gravitated toward in the Northeast had their own versions of the riotous years of the 1960s and '70s, but the demands of adulthood had banked their fires. My friendships in Boston had a tendency to be more distant, less profound. In the predominantly male province of the *Globe* newsroom, where I was hired in the mid-eighties, most of the women I knew were too busy covering wars or politics—sweet cost of victory!—to give much time to close interactions. My independence and solitude gave proof to this: Most of my emotional resources had gone into making my way as a writer, which had solidified my life and maybe even saved it.

I had also realized, gradually but surefootedly, that I didn't want to have children. I had glimpsed this possibility early on, I think, even though I'd grown up in the conservative Texas Panhandle, where marriage and motherhood were as implicit as prayer and football. My parents had each come from large families—my father the ninth of ten, my mother the oldest of six—and their crowded childhoods had convinced them of the calmer luxury of having a small family. My mother, Ruby, had a younger sibling hoisted on her hip throughout her youth, and I suspect she was weary of the job by the time she left the farm, at eighteen, during the height of the Great Depression. She'd made her way in the workforce for a decade before marrying my dad, then waited until her late thirties to have children—a radical gesture for mid-twentieth-century America. She celebrated any route toward contentment: When my sister had her daughter, Ruby was out of her mind with joy; when I left Texas for the East and became a writer, she acted as though I'd climbed Kilimanjaro.

Whatever alternate paths my mother may have envisioned for me, feminism broadened into a four-lane highway. I knew a number of women whose emotional choices were closely linked to the idea of motherhood; because that wasn't a piece of my particular dream, I was free to base my mating calls on love alone. As part of the great wave of women who no longer needed to marry for social or economic status or for children, I had liberated myself right into the wide, bland pastures of noncommitment. This was the good news and occasionally the bad. I'd made my little odyssey to the East alone and unencumbered, and I knew I'd avoided the yoke of an unhappy marriage or being hostage to someone else's paycheck. On my better days, I could feel free and tough and proud of myself; on the bad ones, I was alone as hell. Sick of my Calvinist fortitude, an old friend in Texas sent me a postcard on which she'd scribbled a three-word imperative: "LOWER YOUR STANDARDS."

Thrilling or tiresome, single women's love narratives tend to be desultory stories: Reader, I moved on. I'd had several relationships through my twenties and thirties that ranged from high drama to cosmic misfires, but they belonged to the same era as my rabble-rouser freedom—they were fleeting and fierce, or faux revolutionary and unfulfilling, or decent matches with bad timing. Most of them were wrapped in the amber mist of alcohol, which meant that they rarely stood a chance of trumping my affection for the bottle. With whiskey in the picture, it was always a ménage à trois.

Even for a while after I got sober, I had a tendency to choose passionately and badly. I laughed off the advances of a young reporter who'd been hanging around my desk at the *Globe* until he got a foreign bureau assignment; as soon as I learned he was heading for a hot zone in six weeks, where he would be stationed for years, I had an affair with him. Then I met a journalist for a big-city daily who lived five hundred miles away; when he told me he was suffering shell shock from a bad divorce, I decided we were meant for each other.

If they weren't unavailable or leaving the country, I favored the Pygmalion slow-death trap: choosing a wise, usually narcissistic mentor who wanted to pull me into his orbit. My last serious relationship, with a man named Sam who was a decade older, had fit this template so thoroughly that it probably rid me of the inclination forever. We spent two years together, a small eternity of good and bad, and while I like to believe I would have summoned the strength to leave him of my own accord, his moving to another city was what finally broke the spell.

The night I left him I said goodbye in a crowded airport, tears streaming down my face, then boarded a late shuttle back to Boston. When I woke up the next morning, instead of feeling shattered, I felt safe for the first time in months. The sensation was physical, as though I'd just gotten off a sickening sailboat ride through bad weather. I had to go to a holiday party that evening, and I put on a velvet shirt and cowboy boots and threw cold water on my face. When the hostess met me at the door, she furrowed her brow with worry, and so I said, simply, "I left him."

"Are you all right?" she asked me.

"No," I said, my no longer tragic smile in place. "But I will be."

I found myself a good therapist: a soft-spoken man so largehearted and inimitably wry that my initial fondness for him very soon grew to include trust. He was a Jewish kid from Brooklyn who quoted to me from Baudelaire and the Song of Solomon; he laughed at my jokes, but he didn't laugh when I was being a wiseass to hide my pain. When I wept and told him I was afraid I was too intense, too much, he interrupted my tears and said, "If someone came down from above and told me I could keep only *one thing* about you, it would be your too-muchness."

So began one of the finest connections of my life, which charted, sometimes guided, my navigation toward the light. I turned forty and quit smoking—a twenty-year pack-a-day habit—two days later. My life seemed spartan but solid: If Freud promised work and love to the well-integrated soul, I was attempting a modern-day version of both. The work sustained me; the love belonged to a constellation of friends instead of the trials

and consolations of a romantic partner. It was a bit hard
on the bones at night, but the rock I had climbed onto at
this point in the journey still had a pretty good view.

...

AND THEN, IN THE SPRING OF 1995, CAME A DOG
named Clementine—an experience so emotionally humbling that it rocked my austere world. I had wanted a
Samoyed for as long as I could remember—I even found
an old training guide for the breed, a book that I'd had as
a child—but because they were large sled dogs, I'd assumed it would be unfair to keep one in the city; I was
also loath to leave a dog alone while I spent long days
in the newsroom. Around the same time that I started
working at home, my downstairs neighbors, a young sur-
geon and a lawyer, brought home an eight-week-old
Labrador retriever puppy. I offered to look in on her during the day and soon got into the habit of carrying her
upstairs each morning. She would sleep in my lap while I
read, an arrangement of such mutual reward that it opened
the door onto my old sled dog fantasy. My aging Persian
cat tolerated the Lab, a reception that convinced me I
could introduce another puppy into his domain. So
began a Samoyed research expedition that took me all
over New England. I talked to dog trainers who assured
me it was acceptable to have a Sam in the city; I sought
out breed rescue and breeder-referral people who grilled

me to determine whether I would measure up. Whenever I saw a Samoyed being walked on the street, I stopped its owner and pestered him or her with questions. I drove a hundred miles to see a breeder whose blue ribbon dogs were national champions; her kennels were so crowded and obviously profit-oriented that I fled in distress. Then I went to Connecticut; more grilling, this round made pleasurable by the five adult Samoyeds vying for space in my lap. Finally, after a series of mishaps and unexpectedly small litters, I found a woman in upstate New York with a five-week-old litter of seven. She had a yearlong waiting list for her puppies, she told me, but someone had dropped out that morning, two hours before I called. I've never known whether this was fate or good salesmanship. But two days later, I drove the two hundred miles to Kingston, New York, with a reservation in place at the nearly empty local Holiday Inn. My heart had already left the stratosphere.

That trip was only to *meet* the pups, and to give the breeder a chance to meet me—to see if I was worthy to pair with one of her dogs. Anyone who has taken the labyrinthine journey into the world of purebred dogs will recognize this as a normal course of action from reputable breeders, though for the novitiate, it is both intimidating and thrilling. I've gotten jobs and mortgages more easily than I got Clementine. The breeder had her human candidates choose two puppies, then she matched us with the dog she thought would be the best fit. I chose a feisty trou-

blemaker who had stormed her way onto my lap the moment I met her, and a big, sleepy girl who napped during
most of the visit. I laughed when the breeder called to tell
me I was getting the troublemaker.

Two weeks later, I made the round trip to Kingston
and back in a day, with a friend driving her Saab while I
stayed in the back seat with Clementine, who weighed
eleven pounds and within a year would grow to be five
times that size. I brought her home and began the frantic reorientation that a new animal always ensures: It
seemed as though I had let a wolf cub loose on the place.
She was unstoppable, stubborn, and fearless; when a 120-
pound Irish wolfhound came to visit, Clemmie stood underneath the dog, barking furiously, undaunted by being
outweighed by a factor of ten. After the first sleep-
deprived twenty-four hours of her invasion, I sat on the
back porch with her sprawled asleep in my lap—*She has
white eyelashes!* I thought—and tears started streaming
down my face. I had had animals all my life, but never
had my heart been seized with such unequivocal love.

I UNDERSTOOD THIS attachment for what it was: the
instinctive and deep, probably maternal, feelings for a
being who depends on you for her very survival. My respect for the human-animal connection was well earned;
dogs had always gravitated toward my dad, and I had
grown up with animals. My sister in Texas had an Airedale

and a Border collie. So I was no stranger to cross-species attachments; that mine to Clementine came when and how it did—*single woman, doesn't want kids, loves dogs*—offered a providential answer to the primary relationships that we all require. This mysterious, intelligent animal I had brought into my life seemed to me not a stand-in, but a blessing.

My life changed in the most gratifying and mundane ways. Instead of having dinner out with friends, I joined neighborhood dog groups in the park at night, hanging out with an array of people whose paths weren't likely to cross in a dogless world. An inveterate night owl, I started rising at six a.m. to keep to the housebreaking schedule; my apartment, a once orderly world of old Persian rugs and bookcases, was now littered with squeaky toys and stuffed lemurs. I postponed the idea of the trip abroad I'd been planning and rented a house on a Wellfleet pond instead, where I taught Clementine to swim. Having come of age in the Panhandle, where you could smell the stockyards from ten miles away, I had missed that roughhewn lifestyle ever since I'd moved to the urban Northeast. Now I was back in uniform, in jeans and boots, with dirt on my knees, and I felt as if I'd returned to some long-forgotten place of shelter.

My new friends—the subterranean enclave of dog people—could entertain themselves for hours with talk of fear-aggressive behavior or socialization techniques; if we were seen as insane or tedious by our non-dog friends, we pitied them for what they were missing. Long summer nights were now spent outside, lolling in the fields watching baseball or walking the neighborhood. My priorities had changed, often to the chagrin of others: At a classy soiree in Newton, I irritated my hosts by ignoring the guests and playing in the backyard with their golden retriever. I signed up for obedience classes, then a second round and a third, and looked forward to them all week, reveling in the clarity of communication that training an independent sled dog entailed. Bullying revealed itself immediately for what it was; equally useless were mixed signals, irony, or indecision. Dogs craved and responded to straightforward instruction, recognition, and praise, all of it the direct-arrow language of the heart. For a writer, who spent hours of each day thinking through the intricacies and beauty of words, this link between the species was a place of ease and liberation.

SO WHEN CAROLINE told me, not long after we met, that she was in love with her dog, it didn't require any explanation. While I had been immersed in the challenges of Clementine, Caroline's life was being upended by Lucille, an experience later captured in *Pack of Two*, the book she had just contracted to write. She too had taken on training as though she were undergoing a mission for NASA. I went over to the Concord Armory in Cambridge for two rounds of obedience work with an ex-marine who was convinced Clementine was a blackguard male; every time she misbehaved, he would shout at me, battalion-style, "Tell him he's a rascal!" Caroline was so infatuated with the famous monks of New Skete, New York, masters of German shepherd dogs and the authors of seminal training guides, that she found the monastery's phone number and begged them to let her bring Lucille to visit. We were privately snobbish about our canine knowledge and raised an eyebrow to each other when we saw people making mistakes with their dogs—saying "no" when they meant "stay," or using the "come" command too loosely. But we kept our superiority to ourselves, showing off only to each other. Caroline won the match on the day she saw a soft-coated, pretty ambler at Fresh Pond, and called out to the dog's owner, "Is that a Nova Scotia duck tolling retriever?"

Each of us had this devotion put to the test in the first few months of our friendship: We had coincidentally signed up for the same weeklong session in October at a dog camp in Vermont. Hordes of dog lovers convened at a camp and barracks set on sprawling green acres, where people and dogs got to experience full immersion in training, agility, group meals, and organized play. In the mid-1990s, such places were an anomaly, and Caroline had scoped out the place as an opportunity for research. I was simply there on a lark. It was like a nudist camp for dog lovers, where one might indulge in a natural state away from the inhibiting pressures of normal society. If you wanted to dress your dog in funny costumes, or practice agility with an Afghan hound, no one would laugh at you there, at least not overtly.

From any reasonable perspective, the camp was bedlam. About eighty people and their dogs showed up for the fall session, and the carnival-like atmosphere of the place was probably easier on the humans than on the dogs. Border collies charged around in Frisbee competition, their eyes shining with evangelical focus. Welsh corgis marched up the hill determined as soldiers. I watched my dog run a lure course at what looked to be forty miles an hour; the CBS morning show was there filming, so Clementine had her media day in the sun. Evenings, Caroline and I endured a cafeteria-style supper and then slipped out before the scheduled lectures, heading for our off-site rooms to hash over the absurdities of the day. Near the end of the week, on a group hike over the rolling Vermont terrain, I looked behind me to see some twenty wildly energetic dogs charging up the hill, half of them on retractable leads, their owners trying helplessly to contain them. It looked like a Disney movie gone haywire. Caroline and I sneaked away, found an isolated trail with switchbacks, and let the dogs run. Clementine spotted a deer on the rise and went charging after it; to my astonished joy, she stopped in her tracks when I whistled my long-range recall—she looked down at me, then up toward the deer, and came charging back in my direction. This was enough to convince me that I was doing fine on my own; by then, I'd had enough of the summer camp agenda. I ducked out on the last day's events, forfeited a night at the nearby B&B, and headed for Boston. Caroline, ever the A student, was unnerved but impressed by my mutiny and took it as a cue for her own retreat, though she politely sought out the staff (who couldn't have cared less) to let them know she was leaving.

This was one of the dynamics between us we came to value: She was the good girl and I was the rebel, and each of us learned enough from the other to expand our respective territories. As the daughter of liberal intellectuals who had worshipped Freud and art instead of God, she often complained that she'd had little to rebel against. In the Bible Belt, I'd had a bounty of possible reasons for my insurgency. My mother had come from such a strict Baptist upbringing that she eschewed card-playing on Sunday; my dad was a Nixon Democrat who, protective of his teenage daughters, had patrolled our suburban street with a shotgun—unloaded but effective, particularly when the quarry was a group of adolescent boys. Caroline loved hearing these stories. Her own father, faced with such rivals for his girls, would have brandished a Rorschach test instead of a gun.

THAT AUTUMN WE were walking the fire trails near Sheepfold Meadow at Middlesex Fells; it was a glorious Sunday afternoon, and dozens of people had wandered out of bounds, past the No Trespassing signs near the verboten reservoir, to avail themselves of the view. A town police officer arrived and rounded up only the people with dogs, ignoring the families with strollers and the solitary amblers. He herded us into a queue as though we were a group of delinquents and began writing citations for criminal trespassing. I was planning on using a fake name, which seemed to me the obvious course of action, but Caroline, who was standing in front of me, dutifully announced who she was and where she lived. I sighed and made the decision to go down with her.

A few weeks later we were summoned to court in the neighboring town of Stoneham, where all of us—nineteen offenders—were given a comically harsh lecture for our offense and sentenced to six months' probation. ("Where *is* Stoneham?" Caroline called to ask, the morning before court.) I stood to address the judge and began complaining of discriminatory treatment, as only the dog owners had been cited. The judge made a cursory note of my objection; Caroline looked embarrassed to be with me. Our friend Tom, having seen the particular humor in her being arrested, made her a silk-screened T-shirt with a picture of Lucille behind bars, bearing the legend FREE THE SHEEP-FOLD 19.

KATHY, THE DOG TRAINER who had first told the two of us to get in touch, had done so based on a hunch; she was a deeply intuitive person who spent her days observing dogs and humans for all sorts of behavioral cues. A small, soft-spoken woman who had two German shepherd dogs, she could stop a wayward or dominant dog in its tracks with her calm demeanor and no-nonsense voice. She was equally perceptive with people and had spotted something in Caroline and me before we ever became friends. One day a few months later, when we were at a joint training session in Kathy's backyard, I reached over to fiddle with Caroline's collar and said, "Oh my God, I have that same vest!"

"Of course you do," said Caroline, unimpressed. "Why wouldn't you? We have the same life."

DEEPER THAN MOST of the more obvious parallels between us was the drinking history we had in common—that empty room in the heart that is the essence of addiction. Caroline and I would soon enough tell each other everything, but for the first few months of our friendship, I kept our greatest similarity to myself. The summer before we became friends, I had read Caroline's memoir, *Drinking: A Love Story,* in a rain-soaked cabin in Truro, on Cape Cod, where I had gone for a week with Clementine. I would swim the ponds during the day and read on the screened-in porch until twilight, and I still remember sitting there, Clemmie sleeping next to me, while I read the book until dusk turned to pitch black outside. It was the season of the first round of celebrity addiction memoirs, when Pete Hamill and a few others had come out with new tough-guy versions of *Under the Volcano*. Until now, though, most of the drinking stories had belonged to a boys' club. That night in Truro, I read Caroline's book straight through. I knew it was wrenching, honest, and revelatory. And because I'd poured my last quart of Jack Daniel's down the kitchen sink twelve years earlier, I also knew that it was true.

4.

BY THE TIME I HAD MOVED EAST, IN 1981, THE DRINK-
ing had revealed itself as panacea and problem both,
though I didn't yet see that one almost guaranteed the
other. I came from a line of Texas Protestant bourbon
lovers who had incorporated their affection for whiskey
into a way of life. One exception, at least as I understood
it, had been my maternal grandfather, a sweet blue-eyed
farmer who sang a cappella in the church choir and
pleasantly deferred to my intrepid grandmother's every
wish. Years after they had died, I asked my mother to
confirm what I had always perceived as a harmonious
union.

"Were Mamaw and Granddad happy?" I asked.

"Why, sure," she said. "After Daddy quit drinking."

I was stunned; I had no memory of my granddad ever
touching alcohol. But my mother told me that day about
a summer when I was about four: When we were visiting
our grandparents' farm near Breckenridge, Texas, Grand-

dad had infuriated my father by taking me and my sister to a bar on his way home from errands in town. His binges had been infrequent but legendary, my mother said. He would drink like a wild man for a few weeks, then reappear in church and stay sober for months at a time. After raising six kids in the shadow of this behavior, Mamaw finally threatened to leave him. He stopped drinking shortly thereafter, and because I had been so young at the time, I remembered him only as a teetotaler.

The rest of the family tree had a root system soggy with alcohol, and the memories were not so opaque as with Granddad. One aunt had fallen asleep with her face in the mashed potatoes at Thanksgiving dinner; another's fondness for Coors was so unwavering that I can still remember the musky smell of the beer and the coldness of the cans. Most of the men drank the way all Texas men drank, or so I believed, which meant that they were tough guys who could hold their liquor until they couldn't anymore—a capacity that often led to some cloudy version of doom, be it financial ruin or suicide or the lesser betrayal of simple estrangement. Both social drinkers, my parents had eluded these tragic endings; in the postwar Texas of suburbs and cocktails, their drinking was routine but undramatic.

From my first experiment with drinking at an overnight slumber party, when I was thirteen or fourteen, it was clear I would be lining up with the blackguards in the family. Our young hostess mixed us a noxious blend of scotch and Diet-Rite cola; every other girl had just enough to get goofy or sleepy. I had six tumblers of the stuff, then got on the dining room table to dance while my placid friends snoozed around me. Barely on the verge of adolescence, I was still a shy girl who preferred math homework to boys. I was neither daring nor particularly unhappy, but booze flipped a switch in me I hadn't even known was there.

By high school I was known for having a hollow leg. A good friend told me what the circulated story was on me. " 'Caldwell is the most expensive date in town,' " he quoted the other boys as saying. " 'She'll drink you under the table and she'll never put out.' " My dad would have no doubt appreciated both traits as signs of character. In some of my earliest memories, he had ended his days with a cut-crystal glass of bourbon and Coke, and this magic concoction seemed to make his humor mellow and his voice a little more velvety. By the time he had switched to bourbon and branch water, as he called it, I was a brainy, wild teenager in a macho Texas town, and as much as I fought my dad, I also emulated him. Whiskey took an ordinarily rebellious adolescence and sheathed it in golden light. I had a fake ID at sixteen; on my twenty-first birthday, I became a daily drinker. By then I had wandered through college and the antiwar movement and tried every drug and insurrection in sight, but the pendulum always swung back to the sweet promises of booze. Whenever I would go home to Amarillo, my father would stock the liquor cabinet with scotch and bourbon, then tell me to show some restraint—the excellent duplicity of Texas drinking etiquette, which counseled that you drink like a man and act like a lady. "There are two things a man can't stand," my dad would say after our first couple of belts, his voice gravelly and full of self-satisfied wisdom. "A woman with round heels, and a woman who drinks too much." We would both nod sagely, and I would ask him to explain the first part. He would make a pushing motion with his hand and shake his head. For years I thought that round-heeled meant spineless, because he was too modest ever to explain it.

But he always knew, I think, that drinking was going to be my problem. He knew because I got too happy and animated even at the sight of a drink, and because he shared this dark affection and yet had managed to cap the geyser at its source. If half the people on both sides of our extended family had loved the drink too much, I tended to laugh about it because I couldn't bear to consider the consequences. My relatives also had a constitution that allowed them to live well into their nineties, and in the calculus of denial, I used this longevity to counterbalance our affliction. "In my family," I used to say, "if alcoholism or suicide doesn't get you, you'll live forever."

I usually said this with a tumbler of whiskey in my hand. ("But you always just had that one glass," my sister said, years after I had stopped, when she was trying to piece together the mosaic of the past. "Yes," I told her, "and it was always full.") Because my tolerance allowed me to drink hugely but functionally for years—I survived most of graduate school with a cache of scotch—I culti- vated an image that waffled between tragedy and libera- tion. The self-perception was constructed to fit the need: With alcohol the mandatory elixir, I would erect a stage set to justify its presence. I would be the sensitive hero- ine, or doomed romantic, or radical bohemian—I was Hamlet, Icarus, Edith Wharton's Lily Bart. God forbid that I simply face who I was, which was somebody drunk and scared and on my way to being no one at all.

Most of this self-actualization was unfolding in Austin in the 1970s, when the streets flowed with cocaine and whiskey; I surrounded myself, unconsciously but probably intentionally, with people who drank the way I did. Some of them got straight and some of them died, and a few of them calmed down, grew up, and settled for one martini instead of seven. I did my part for my gener- ation's collective crisis of adulthood by moving east, with the brazen notion of becoming a writer—surely, accord- ing to myth, a way to reinvent one's life. When I left Texas, I had two quarts of whiskey in the trunk of my old Volvo, which I figured would cover the five days on the road that were ahead of me. I had a few friends in New York and knew two people in Greater Boston, where I was going, and however scared I was, I knew there would be a liquor store wherever I landed. By then I was thirty years old, and I'd learned that courage in a bottle could get you through all kinds of doors, and all kinds of trouble, and a lot of dead-end nights alone.

In the early 1980s, hordes of people were leaving the Northeast for the softer industries and climates of the Sun Belt. New England was cold, dark, and unforgiving, people warned me; the more precarious truth was that I had no job, no place to live, and enough savings to last a year. My writing résumé consisted of a couple of rejection slips from venerated magazines; my confidence came from a few gruff encouragements from professors. But however fragile the external scaffolding looked, I suspect that I was trying to save my life, not just relocate it. I had grown up staring at the vast, imprisoning horizon of the Texas Panhandle, a region I understood how much I loved only long after I had left it, and I had jumped free of that place with a kind of high-octane terror. If conservative Amarillo, with its oil rigs and churches and cattle ranches, promised a provincial life, for years I challenged every dictum I perceived my family to possess. A decade later, I had to assume an equally resolute posture to get out of Austin—to leave behind what I loved and what I feared was killing me.

I was equal parts bluff and fear, I think, poised there on the verge of a life unfolding, not knowing whether I would leap or fall. In my last couple of years in Austin, when I had been teaching at the university and pretending to read for doctoral oral exams, I had let my heart lead me to the water's edge of a writing life—an inner sanctum of such power and solace that it staggered me with its reach. I lived in a few rooms of an old southern mansion with ten-foot ceilings and poured-glass windows, and I would sit there at night before my typewriter, primed with a glass of scotch and a pack of Winstons. One night before the drink kicked in I had written something that so excited me—I have no memory of what it was—that I leapt up from my chair and kept typing standing up. Probably every young would-be writer has such moments, the crystal-clear elation that keeps one going. But now I see the moment as pivotal and even Faustian: the amber light, the whirring typewriter, the young woman full of yearning and joy. The writing was the life force and the whiskey was the snake in the grass. For as long as I could, I chose them both.

YOUTH AND PRIDE can be decent weapons against the woes of alcohol, but only for a while. I kept jobs, I threw cold water on my face each morning, I swam laps to counter the effects of the booze and then drank to wipe out the gains of the swim. For years the psychic balm of alcohol—its holy grail certainty that it could take me through anything—eclipsed the hangovers and emerging fear that I was in trouble. I had a silver pocket flask that I filled with whiskey for backup drinks; I figured if I looked the part, then I could get away with the reality.

The booze took the rough corners off, and I tried to right the equation with coffee and protein and five milligrams of Librium to ease the comedown. I was a well-oiled machine, with a 4.0 grade-point average, and nobody knew. Or so I believed.

Why did I drink? When my therapist asked me this several years after I had stopped, I thought it one of the most ludicrous questions I had ever heard. Why *wouldn't* one drink? I didn't want to hurt his feelings, so I shrugged and answered as honestly as I knew how. "Be*cauuse*," I said, with a little scorn. "The whole world turned golden." It took me hearing the words out loud to realize that the hue of the sublime had itself been an indicator of trouble.

A few professionals over the years had made feeble efforts to address the problem; in Texas in the 1970s, "substance abuse" wasn't even a phrase yet. My last couple of years in graduate school, I went to see a nice woman psychologist to address, or so I thought, the ordinary stresses of work and love: I was in a demanding academic program, I had just broken up with someone, I was having difficulty sleeping. We ate Milano cookies together, the therapist and I, and laughed about how hard life was. "I think I drink too much," I said one day. "I'm throwing down five or six glasses of whiskey a night. Maybe I need to check in to Shoal Creek." Shoal Creek was the psych hospital in Austin where people went to dry out; a lawyer I'd worked for (and who taught me how to drink scotch and eat raw oysters) had considered it his spa. "They

wouldn't take you," my lovely, nonconfrontational therapist said. "You look too good."

By which she meant that I was still vertical, still
functioning in superdrive, and that I hadn't yet had the
external calamities that suggested a problem: no drunk
driving citations, crashed marriages, employment woes.
The same year I had a routine physical with a male internist who was less benevolent and more obtuse. When
he asked me how much I drank, I told him about four
drinks a night, not yet aware that the medical profession's
rule of thumb, if a patient's consumption seemed prob-
lematic, was to double whatever quantity the patient
confessed. "You'll want to be careful with that," he said,
refusing to look me in the eye. "There's nothing more
unbecoming than a young lady who drinks too much."

Such idiocies only fueled my intake. I was in my late
twenties by then, a veteran of the counterculture and the
women's movement, and I clung to the belief that my
drinking was part of the sine qua non of a new day—it
was how women like me functioned in the world; it was
an anesthetic for high-strung sensitivity and a lubricant
for creativity. The alternative truth was far grimmer.
Alcoholics—a word I couldn't even think of without
shame and terror—were broken people who had drunk
themselves into a corner, and the only way out for them
was to give up the drink. That was unthinkable to me,
a gray, gray room without any highs or relief or even

change, and so I clung for years to what I believed was the border between alcoholism and drinking to excess. Every time I voiced my fears it was in the guise of humor, or machismo, or nonchalant rebellion. "I'm afraid that if I stopped drinking, I wouldn't be interesting anymore," I said offhandedly to a friend in Austin, an RN whose father had died of alcoholism after sitting in a chair surrounded by beer cans for decades. "Don't be so sure," she told me. "Day in and day out, boring is where all alcoholics are headed."

No one whose first allegiance is to the source of the problem can hear such warnings, at least not until they've dragged themselves through a few miles of broken glass. Help in its most benign and unthreatening form—if there is even such a thing for an alcoholic—wasn't exactly beating down the door; if it had, I'd probably have moved out in the middle of the night. I didn't want help; I wanted reassurance. Which is to say that I wanted the consolation, however transient or artificial, that I would be able to drink forever and get away with it. It's like the old joke about the guy on the desert island with the genie who offers him two wishes. The guy asks for a bottle of beer. The genie instantly produces, and tells the man that the bottle will never be empty and will always be cold, and that he still has one more wish. Just to be sure, the man tells the genie, you'd better give me another one.

WHEN I WAS STILL young and brave enough to crave adventure, I came to the East Coast. I had been an adult the first time I'd ever set foot in New York, a few years earlier, and the city had offered the usual elixir. I walked eighty blocks, from the Guggenheim Museum to Greenwich Village, in a daze of happiness. I stood on a corner amid whirling snow and fleets of cabs and all the other pop culture icons that I had grown up seeing on movie and TV screens; the idea that these things were real—that you could walk into this luminous scene and become a part of it—was humbling and life-altering. I went to the Museum of Modern Art, where Picasso's *Guernica* was still housed, and I had to hang on to the railing when I turned on the stairs and saw it for the first time. However sophisticated I deemed myself to be, I had grown up with wheat fields and suburbs as the visual constant, with art as something that mostly belonged in books. Being in Manhattan was like running headlong toward your own life, or finding out you could fly. To turn away from it would have seemed the failure of a chance not taken.

Cambridge had its own gorgeous, if more reserved, version of seduction. On my first trip there I had gone to the Orson Welles Cinema, with its arty documentaries and cappuccino machine, and I'd wandered through Harvard Yard in a battered leather jacket, trying to pass as a local—sensing, I think, that I had found a place far greater and more consuming than the confines of my own sad heart. Maybe this is a common perception of youth, holding back fear with exhilaration. But I look back now and see myself as shadows bumping into light. The light was trying its damnedest to win, and part of the plan, I believed, was to get out of Texas.

THAT FIRST SUMMER in New England, I lived in a sprawling three-story house with six other people. The household included a physician, a physicist, a dancer, and a couple of puppet makers, and somehow this glamorous cast found me exotic—partly, I feel sure, because of the hard-drinking image I was still trying to pull off. I had the boots and macho countenance and two bottles of whiskey I kept in brown bags on a closet shelf, and my housemates seemed amused by the drawling Texan who had invaded their genteel counterculture. My closest friend in the house was Jackie, the dancer, who attired herself for a normal outing in faux leopard hats and pink elbow gloves, and each evening at the dinner table would begin the recitation of her day by saying, "First, I got up!" We adored each other—she was the revolutionary Dr. Joyce Brothers to my tragic heroine—and one afternoon, the day after a summer party at the house, we were sprawled in the backyard, comparing notes. I had a worse hangover than usual, and in a moment of candor, said so. Besides being a dancer and an eccentric, Jackie was also an RN; she had worked in the trenches of the medical field and seen the psychic casualties of the sixties and seventies. We were lying next to each other with our eyes closed—the peer-analytic position—and out of the blue she said, "Are you an alcoholic?"

She might as well have been asking if I were a Pisces, the question was so gentle. And I was so surprised that I answered honestly. "I don't know," I told her. "I know that I'm psychologically addicted."

The exchange hovered through my consciousness for the next three years I would drink. Jackie had dared to ask what I could not; my answer had let someone else in the room with all that fear, if only for a minute. A few months later, I moved down the street to an attic garret, a place with all the romantic underpinnings of the life I hoped to lead and all the bleak corners of what I first had to leave behind. Jackie had the foresight and kindness to understand this darkness and stay nearby while I lived through it. I braved the streets of Boston, landed some freelance writing assignments, came home and poured down drinks while I hammered away on the Adler type-writer. I got a Persian kitten and named him Dashiell Hammett, and he sat on the pillows of my bed while I drank, his huge eyes witness to the staggering and the late-night blackouts I couldn't stand to endure alone. The *Phoenix,* an alternative newspaper in Boston, took me on as a regular contributor, and I wrote my columns in the light of morning when I was sober; if I was a drunk, I was also a perfectionist—two traits, I believed, that would ultimately balance each other out. I smuggled pamphlets on alcoholism out of a doctor's office and took the twenty-question test with a glass of bourbon in my hand. In the early 1980s, the questions still made traditional social assumptions about women; one of them, unforgettably, was "Have your husband and children ever expressed concern about your drinking?" I checked off "No" with a flourish. No husband, no children, no worries.

The more looming truth was that what had seemed like liberation—the flight from Texas, the brown bags of whiskey, the reinvention of a life—was revealing itself to be unmoored terror. On the advice of an internist, I went to see a psychotherapist and hypnotist who specialized in substance abuse. He placed me in a reclining chair as though I were in a dentist's office, and every time he hypnotized me I began to weep silently, the tears streaming down my face until my hair was wet. This in itself was evidence that some deep sorrow was trying to get out, but the hypnotist seemed to think aversion therapy was in order. He instructed me to go home and drink as much as I possibly could in the following week, then bring him a quart of scotch to pay for our next appointment.

I like to think that my compromised state—the drinking, the soggy trances—was what kept me from fleeing this strange milieu. For weeks I went back, hoping somehow he could hit the magic switch that would end my paralyzed attachment. Then one day he came into the room smiling. He told me that he had taken LSD the previous week and had had a vision of me; he knew now that everything was going to be all right. He went on to describe the sexual infatuation he believed existed between us, one that, he was careful to say, would never be acted on. "On a scale of one to ten," he told me, in a mode of cheerful confession, "you're about a nine." After assuring him that this numeric affection belonged to him alone, I fled. I never paid the bill he sent me for that last mystical instruction; I never answered his querulous letters. For years I pondered the damage he could have done, or at least the failure he had visited on me.

BECAUSE I HAD the sense and the pride not to drive drunk or appear blasted in public, my world got smaller and smaller. I had bruises on my upper arms from running into doorways; when I sprained my ankle, I tied two plastic bags to the crutch handles—one holding ice, the other, a flask of bourbon—and hobbled with my portable bar from the kitchen to the desk. Then one night I went beyond these amateur foibles and took a fall that landed me in the ER. Standing before the bathroom mirror in one of those Leonard Cohen tragic moments, I had collapsed, dead weight, with a glass of scotch in my hand. I landed crosswise against the bathtub and broke four ribs. It was four a.m. Even to my denial-racked mind, this was no longer social drinking.

The cultural dictates of time and space—of Texas and its drinking culture, of the still provincial understanding about addiction—had always told me that alcoholism was something untreatable and reprehensible. It happened to people who were broken in other ways, or weak, or who didn't have the willpower to straighten up and fly right, as my dad would have said. What this version always left out was the inner struggle—the want for drink trying to eclipse the light of survival—that someone in the throes of addiction endures. Every morning, waking to the sorrows of another night's failures, I would swallow my fear and swear that this time, today, I would have only four drinks. I would switch to vodka, or go to a movie, or call Jackie, who now lived in New York, and tell her how bad it was. The tape would play all day long—courage/terror, resolve/yearning, bargaining/surrender—and then I would crack open the freezer for the ice and my whole body would exhale in relief, and the cycle would start to play itself out again.

The worst psychic legacy of this endless loop was the ongoing feeling of betrayal. Each day I made a contract not to drink, and every night by eight or nine I had broken it again. The erosion, like water on stone, was gradual and constant. I had been blessed with parents whose separate strengths had been passed on to me; I had my mother's independence and my father's tough-minded resolve. And I had a trust in myself that was based on three decades of pretty good outcomes. But this adversary was far crueler, stronger, more persistent than any challenge I had faced. The last year had proven that it was no longer a deadlock; I had actually had a dream that I was in the ring with a bottle of Jack Daniel's and I was being beaten to a pulp. For more than a decade I had negotiated with the gods so that I could keep the booze: Meet the deadline, get the bottle. Get the writing assignment, have the drink. The better I felt about the prose at the end of the day, the greater the reward.

WHICH MIGHT EXPLAIN the cliffwalker behavior I engaged in as a writer, going after stories that I thought would somehow legitimate my intake. I had been scheduled to leave two days after my fall on an assignment to the weather observatory atop Mount Washington in New Hampshire, a moonlike outpost that boasted the worst weather in the world. Because of the broken ribs, I postponed the trip for six weeks. When I made the three-hour bus ride in February to Gorham, New Hampshire, at the base of the mountain, my ribs were still wrapped and I had painkillers and two quarts of whiskey in my luggage. We left Boston at six p.m., and the bus headed north into the dark. I sat on that lonely bus in the cold with my aching ribs and my Percocet, eating a bleak little ham sandwich I had packed for the trip, trying not to think about the frightening state I found myself in. By the time we got to Gorham, the end of the line, there was only one other passenger, a creepy-looking man who made eyes my way and acted as though he might follow me. I got off the bus using a walking stick to navigate the ice and made it to the local hostel, and as soon as I got to my room I threw down eight ounces of bourbon. The next morning when the Sno-Cat arrived to drive me and a couple of geologists up the mountain, I was more worried about the glass bottles I had stashed in my backpack than I was about my own fractured anatomy.

Consciously or inadvertently, I had picked a drinker's hermitic paradise at the observatory. The meteorologists were used to being locked in by inclement weather for weeks at a time, and they had a full liquor reserve along with their gallons of tomato sauce and industrial-size spices. My two housemates gave me a glass-lined office overlooking the ravines of Mount Washington; evenings, we would meet to cook dinner over a few drinks. Their morning shift began at five a.m., so by eight every night I could retire to my bunkbeds and my bottle of bourbon. And every night I made a scratch on the bottle so I could be sure the rations would last.

The next few months were a blur of adrenaline and fear, a last-ditch effort to maintain the facade. I arranged to do a story about Boston Light, one of the last manned lighthouses in America, which entailed my spending the night on Little Brewster Island in Boston Harbor with the lightkeeper and his dog. I still had the morning shakes when the Coast Guard's cigarette boat arrived to take me over to the island. There were three or four sweet, rowdy fellows in the boat, showing off and gunning the engine, and because I didn't want them to see how nervous and sick I was, I employed the old Texas maneuver of raising the stakes. "So," I asked them, "how fast can you guys make this thing go?" They grinned at me and then at one another, and took me across the harbor at about sixty miles per hour. I was pale when I set foot on the island, but they thought I was tough—at least I thought they thought I was tough—and to my addled sense of self, that was what mattered.

But the lightkeeper knew. By now my pride was a tattered camouflage for the problem. At the end of our afternoon together I went upstairs and drank six ounces of vodka in about twenty minutes, then reappeared in the kitchen to watch him cook me a T-bone steak. We were the only people on the island, and he was a big, strapping, shy fellow in his midthirties, and we sat that night in his bright kitchen, drinking Pepsi and eating steak, while he told me a story, seemingly out of nowhere, about how he had given up drinking a few years earlier. I smiled and nodded sympathetically. I had chosen vodka so he wouldn't smell it, but he knew. The next morning, hungover, I forced myself to climb the dizzying steps to the top of the ninety-foot tower, and I made myself count the steps as I went so I could put the number in the story. When people say alcoholics have no willpower, they have no idea.

FOR ALL MY MOCK heroics, my constant recalibrations of the fuel and the facade, I know now that writing is what threw me a rope and let me drag myself to shore: The idea of a world where I kept the drink but lost the writing was even more unbearable to me than one without booze. During those wretched last months, I'd started finding boozy, half-comprehensible notes I had scrawled to myself late at night. By day my sober prose was at least lucid and legible; these notes from the dark side were like coming across an ex-Broadway floozy in a gin palace who had seen better days. I was thirty-three years old. It seemed way too soon for the tragic decline, however much the tortured-romantic myth had driven me onward. I had fostered for years the sodden hall of fame of those writers who lassoed their talent with a bottle of whiskey: Faulkner and Hemingway and Hammett (tellingly, my inner referents were mostly male). What I had conveniently left out of this self-told tale were the endnotes that proved the lie: Faulkner's discipline, Hammett's long sobriety, Hemingway's shotgun. Whiskey didn't stoke the flame of creativity; it extinguished it, sometimes one slow drop at a time.

The garret where I had thought to live out my

writerly fantasy was a third-floor walk-up on a tree-lined city street. My typewriter was in the front room of the apartment, and I could look out the front windows onto rooftops and the New England sky, and below to the street scene of people going about their lives—the mail carriers and dog walkers and familiar strangers that form the background canvas of urban life. One winter afternoon when I was still housebound with broken ribs, wanting nothing more than to walk to the liquor store for a bottle of bourbon, I stood there watching the snow fly outside and my heart seized with the disparity of the dream delivered: I had come here, all this way, with no job or family or scaffolding, intent on making it as a writer, and now I was trapped three floors up in my own little cell block, removed utterly from the people below and waiting for the day to end so I could drink. The free fall I'd been in for years had ended, and the fear had become despair, and I simply couldn't bear it anymore.

VICTORY STORIES ARE usually pretty simple: As I once heard a man in an AA meeting put it, "I got drunk, it got worse, I got here." By spring I had signed up for an alcoholism education class at my Cambridge health plan, where a tall, easygoing fellow named Rich, a few years older than I, talked each week about the ravages of the disease. I thought he was a fool. I would go home after class and pour huge tumblers of bourbon and brood about what he'd said. He was too tall, too kind, too unhip. Clearly there had been some mistake—the medical literature had left out a category for tragic heroines with brilliant futures who loved their whiskey. Then the next week I would stagger back in to continue my education.

My gentle teacher did two things that were invaluable. The first was that he seemed to expect nothing from his audience: He didn't browbeat us or try to herd us into sobriety, or even ask us to come back. The second was that he gave a Buddhist-like interpretation of how to survive life without alcohol that had been left out of every pamphlet I'd ever read. Throughout my drinking I had assumed that the slide into alcoholism was a fait accompli failure—that you'd already lost the battle and were consequently beyond redemption. The best one could hope for, I assumed, was a shaky, vigilant life of bleak anxiety. Rich acceded the battle but none of the rest. The concept of AA, he told us in the final class, was one of surrender. I rolled my eyes; I had heard this before. And, he went on, surrender—deciding to lay down the weapon and walk away from the fight—was a way to get back all your power.

The fluorescent lights softened a little, and that grim classroom where I had sat for weeks with other doubters gave off an aura, however transient, of hope. I recognized what he was talking about: This was the old mythic struggle that had defined heroism throughout the ages. Somehow that night the concept of sobriety, for the first time, had a revolutionary tinge to its message—the idea was life-saving, anti-mainstream, even daring. It might be possible, I thought that night, to give up drinking *and still be cool.* For a frightened young woman who'd spent a decade cultivating an au courant armor to mask her drinking, this was as radical as it got.

He saved my life, of course, this compassionate, low-key man who didn't give a whit about being cool but cared tremendously about helping people. Having laid down my defense of disdain, I went to see him one afternoon after the class was over, with the ostensible purpose of talking about the alcoholism in my extended family. And even though I was cold sober that day, afterward I remembered almost nothing from the hour we spent in Rich's office. I know that in the first few minutes I broke down, to my own horror, and said, "I think I drink too much." The rest was a wash of memory, until he got up nearly an hour later and rushed out to schedule me for outpatient detox the following week. Months later, I asked him about that day and what I had said. He smiled, having seen this amnesia-in-crisis before. "Mostly," he told me, "you tried to convince me that you weren't worth saving."

This shocks me now as it did then, because I always

clung to the flicker of self-regard that I assumed got me in to see him. But alcohol, and the desperation and exhaustion that went along with it, had so worn me down that I didn't have much fight left in me. I went home that day to finish a deadline for the *Village Voice*. Then I drove to the neighborhood liquor store for what I hoped would be my last stash. I got a quart of Jack Daniel's and— a splurge, on my freelancer's income—a quart of Johnnie Walker Red. "Would you like the gift box?" the innocent cashier asked me. "Sure," I told her. "Why not?" Three days later, I poured what was left down the sink and staggered into Rich's office, hungover and half an hour late, for an appointment that would let me start again.

IT WAS THE SUMMER of 1984, and AA in those days was still removed from the social order—it hadn't yet hit the covers of the newsweeklies, the slogans hadn't been turned into bumper stickers, and celebrity redemption confessions were a thing of the future. Armed with a schedule of local meetings, I slunk into a Cambridge meeting a few days before my last drink and sat weeping near the back until a soft-voiced, elegant woman elbowed me in the ribs and whispered, "Don't worry—it's biochemical." I found this uplifting: a four-word answer, delivered casually but unequivocally, to the biggest problem in my life. I left there and went home to the Johnnie

Walker, but I went back the next night, and the next, and by the time Monday morning had rolled around and I was scheduled to be back in Rich's office for my syllabus of a new life, I had finished the scotch, thrown in a lot of bourbon just to be sure, and hauled a bar's worth of empty bottles down to the street.

Partly because twelve-step programs hadn't yet saturated the culture, the meetings I went to seemed clandestine and hardscrabble; most of them were held in church basements. There was something incredibly romantic about this—it was like being a Mason with a bad rap sheet. In graduate school I had been immersed in the memoirs of writers who had joined the Communist Party in the 1930s and who stole around to secret meetings of their cell groups, smoking and talking and convinced they were changing the world. I'd always envied their passionate focus. One summer evening I was crossing the Boston Common toward another church basement, with the grounds full of people on their way somewhere. For years I had felt removed from this stream of humanity, charging toward moments of what seemed like a realized life. Now I knew the deeper, more varied truth: that a few members of the crowd were headed to an AA meeting. This was a hard-won but brilliant education: I had realized, as life is always willing to instruct, that the world as we see it is only the published version. The subterranean realms, whether churches or hospital rooms or smoke-filled basements, are part of what hold up the rest. I had gotten ahold of a skeleton key and found my way inside.

I'D KNOWN SOMEONE in Austin, years before, who had joined AA and put her life back together, but what no one could have told me was how uproariously funny the meetings were. I walked into shabby rooms with folding chairs and coffee urns, where people were getting sugar fixes on grocery-store cookies and using old tuna cans as ashtrays. A people's tribunal of drunks! AA cut across every class line I had ever hoped to breach. There were men in business suits and tough-talking blue-collar women and diffident souls you'd overlook on a subway train; there were scary-looking guys who, once they started talking, you'd have wanted to have your back forever. The stories they told were wrenching and outrageous and sometimes profound, and for the most part they had happier outcomes, at least so far, than what you could expect from a lot of life. I made friends with a beautiful young woman, an artist and filmmaker, who shredded Styrofoam cups throughout the meetings; she did this for about a year, while I chain-smoked next to her. She had discovered the magic Molotov cocktail that was alcohol when she was barely an adolescent, and had recently graduated magna cum laude from Harvard while nearly drinking herself to death. For years we hung out in the front rows of the meetings together, fancying ourselves the Thelma and Louise of Cambridge AA, until her work took her to New York, where she belonged. Eliza was tough, but inside was a woman of such gentleness and depth that she could lower my blood pressure just by walking into the room. She too had found her way to AA through the Benevolent Alcohol Counselor, and for years we referred to ourselves as graduates of the Rich Caplan Finishing School, where we had learned the careful etiquette of how to avoid consuming a quart of whiskey in one sitting, or at all.

I USED TO THINK this was an awful story—shameful and dramatic and sad. I don't think that anymore. Now I just think it's human, which is why I decided to tell it. And for all the wise words about drinking heard and forgotten over the years, particularly that first blurred hour in Rich's office, I've always remembered one thing he said that day, when I was buried in fear and shame at the idea that I had drunk my way into alcoholism. He asked me why I was so frightened, and I told him, weeping, the first thing that came into my mind: "I'm afraid that no one will ever love me again." He leaned toward me with a smile of great kindness on his face, his hands clasped in front of him. "Don't you *know*?" he asked gently. "The flaw is the thing we love."

5.

SOME OF THE EFFECTS OF STOPPING DRINKING WERE immediate and dramatic. I cleaned the house, swam a mile every day, nursed my newfound craving for sugar. I went to scores of AA meetings and read stacks of novels at night when I couldn't sleep. I got a job as an editor at a local literary review, where on the first day of work I met Matthew, a tall, gentle man with a timbre-rich voice who became a good friend, and who seemed to personify my life of second chances—with him, the world had turned from an obstacle course into an amusement park. Matthew and I would sit in the office late into the evening, smoking and reading the slush pile of unsolicited manuscripts while the snow flew outside the windows overlooking Mass Ave. Six months later, *The Boston Globe* hired me as its underling book critic. The first day in the newsroom, my colleagues presented me with a bottle of champagne, a civility so unnerving that I carried it to the trunk of my car that night as though it were plutonium, then unloaded it at a friend's house on the way home. In 1985, the reputation of the newsroom as a hard-drinking place was still well earned, and I was just learning the skill of meeting deadlines without a drink at the end of the day. One night I asked a fellow critic how he landed the plane after he had filed. "Oh, I just go home and have a few scotches and a couple of Librium," he told me. "That pretty much does it for me." I lit another cigarette, filed the review I was writing, and went to an AA meeting.

The self becoming: In my first year of sobriety, I heard a woman at an AA meeting describe the day in, day out pact with tedium and despair that alcoholism had meant for her. "I would go out and live my life," she said, "and then come home at the end of the day and drink six beers to make it all go away. It was like covering a blackboard with writing every morning and then that night erasing everything you'd learned."

This story stayed with me as a mantra and an explanation. What I couldn't have known, in the drinking years, was that alcohol was my shortcut to the stars, and that there are no shortcuts, not without a price. The drink had salved, not solved the problems; it had blurred the lessons of a bad day or a celebration or any of the incremental turtle steps that constitute experience. To allow myself to drink all those years and not go mad with the psychic damage I was inflicting, I created a whiskey-tinged artifice that sweetened the myth. Now I had laid down the props, and as terrifying as this was, it was also a little like releasing a helium balloon. I had no idea the world could be so light, the flight so internally propelled.

Still, my walking through fire didn't stop overnight. When I was a couple of months sober I had proposed an essay to the *Globe Magazine* about the seamier side of Atlantic City, and gone there and stayed up half the night playing blackjack, drinking club soda at the tables at three a.m. while waitresses plied the gamblers with free booze. My sponsor in AA had pointed out the foolishness of this maneuver, but I made it home unscathed, particularly after witnessing the predawn wreckage that prowled the casinos. But if the need for such mock heroics waned over the next few years, I was still horrified at the idea of people finding out I was an alcoholic. And on some level I still believed that people who could drink socially had access to a private club of risk-free, glistening highs from which I had been forever barred.

This is a dangerous myth for an alcoholic, though I suppose we all have some version of it, the old Gatsby spin in which the light through the windows is always more enchanting when viewed from the street outside. It's the common equation of yearning, and God did I yearn: for bourbon, for the magazine ad life that attended it, for the golden, ever-elusive balm that had stoked the fires of addiction from the beginning. One night I had to go to a tony dinner party that epitomized these images: the elegant house, the bar in the library, the seemingly dazzling table talk and constant flow of wine. I was the only person not drinking, and after consuming great quantities of Perrier, I got in my car at midnight and collapsed. In tears, I called a friend who was a late-night DJ and always awake in the wee hours. "Those people don't *matter*," he said to me. "You're stronger and better than all those people." This was the same man who, with care and patience, had listened a year earlier when I was contemplating life without alcohol. "I'm afraid that if I stop drinking, I'll be dreary, and anxious all the time, and dull," I had told him. "Well, you might be," he had said matter-of-factly. "The only thing you can know for sure is that you'll be a whole lot less drunk."

After a while, a whole lot less drunk was what I aspired to be. I learned to navigate the alcohol-sodden social terrain and sometimes avoid it altogether; what had once beckoned as a charmed life became less enviable over time, and even alien. I knew something fundamental had shifted one night in downtown Boston, where I was part of a welcoming group for a visiting luminary. We met at the Ritz-Carlton, and everyone else—all of them men—ordered two-fisted drinks of Polish vodkas and double scotches. I smiled at the waiter. "What sort of designer water do you have?" I asked, and after he'd taken our order, the luminary cast me a look of scorn. "You don't *drink?*" he said. "How boring."

"Not to me, it isn't," I shot back. Rather than feeling exposed as the fragile woman with the club soda, I was instead stunned by the man's rudeness. I had stopped caring what he, or maybe anyone, thought.

BY THE TIME Caroline and I became friends, we were each fairly well out of the corridors of isolation that went along with alcoholic drinking. She'd been sober a couple of years and was trying to maintain her footing, particularly given the exposure that *Drinking: A Love Story* had received. Some of this publicity had been as absurd as it was grueling: One TV news crew tried to arrange an interview in a bar, then asked her if she could cry on camera. I had more than a decade's worth of meetings and sobriety behind me—we had both stopped drinking when we were thirty-three—and I could well remember those early, new-colt efforts at reorienting a life. But while Caroline had, in many ways, protected herself by going public, I had chosen the opposite path; the only people who knew what I'd been through were close friends and family. Because I hadn't wanted her candor to dictate my own disclosures, I waited months into our friendship before I told her. I was sitting in her living room one autumn afternoon and said, "There's something I need to tell you," and she looked apprehensive— *What have I done wrong?*—and I smiled at her worry and said, "This probably won't surprise you, but I haven't had a drink in twelve years."

The look on her face was of relief and happy surprise,

the oh-my-God smile of connection. Months later, we were talking about the night we'd first met years before, when we had been foisted on each other at a party. Unbeknownst to her, I had been sober several years by then. "I remember how shy you were," I said. She laughed at her memory of me, even though I had been holding a glass of club soda at the time. "I remember thinking," she told me, "that here was a woman who could probably drink the way she wanted to and get away with it."

So much for first impressions; that was one of the few times I saw Caroline's instincts about people fail her. If our individual pasts with alcohol were familiar, the more intricate and lasting truth we shared was about the ability to change—the belief that life was hard and often its worst battles were fought in private, that it was possible to walk through fear and come out scorched but still breathing. This was the melancholic's version of hope, but a studied one, and we carried it with us whether confronted with real difficulties or the mundane fender benders of life. Caroline had rowed her way out of anorexia in her late twenties; I had crawled and then limped my way out of polio. That long climb had made me both determined and stubborn, traits that had been essential to my getting sober. Because Caroline and I recognized in each other this mode of survival, we gave each other wide berth—it was far easier, we learned over the years, to be kind to the other than to ourselves. When Caroline insisted that she walk Lucille four miles, I assured her that

two was plenty; when I insisted on trying to lift an un-
wieldy thirty-five-pound boat over my head on a down-
ward ramp, she drove to the boathouse to help me carry
it. We named the cruel inner taskmaster we each possessed the Inner Marine, which took away the sting
when I got beaten on the river or she wore out in the
pool, and we invented the character of Sarah Tonin to
personify our quasi-dramatic selves. Each gave the other
permission to lower the bar—I would call her from the
boathouse when the wind was fierce, and she would convince me *not* to row. This latitude extended to our self-
doubts about the lives we had chosen, the ambivalence
we shared about being moody introverts who often preferred the company of dogs. One night when Caroline
was making tea in her kitchen alone, she was flooded
with a sense of well-being. She reported this the next
morning with a sort of confessional delight. "Oh my
God, I'm the merry recluse!" she told me she had said
aloud. "And Gail is the cheerful depressive!"

As usual, Caroline got a column out of that evening's
epiphany—the merry recluse became a character in her
print chronicle of her own fears. "Is there a column in
this?" she would ask in the middle of a conversation
funny or profound, her ever-present omniscient narrator
trolling for material. Like most friends of writers, I found
this dual scrutiny by turns flattering, amusing, and irri-
tating, even though Caroline went to great lengths to
protect her subjects' privacy. One of the worst fights we

ever had happened after she had lent me her boat to row on an October morning. Pulling the scull out of the cold, murky Charles River, I had lost my footing, and the boat's sliding seat had come off its tracks and gone flying into the river.

I was heartsick at my clumsiness, and Caroline had to talk me out of diving into the filthy river to search for the seat. "It's not like you lost *Lucille*," she consoled me, but she was still annoyed, and it took us both days to recover. She was exasperated that I had put the boat out of commission for a couple of weeks; I was upset that she was upset. But the later dissonance came in Caroline's effort to disguise me. When she wrote about this tempest—an essay about intimacy and conflict for a women's magazine—she turned the lost object into a pair of gold earrings. Now I was the one who was annoyed, even though no one in a million years would mistake me for an earring borrower. I was angry because I thought that in trying to grant the essay a wider appeal, she had traded down our tools. We didn't borrow jewelry; we took it off or stopped wearing it altogether. Masters of our own universe, we were, a country small and self-determined.

For me the territory had been hard won, which is one reason I was so protective of it. The younger daughter of a warm-hearted Texas patriarch, I had adored my father and, in the classic Oedipal dance, had tried to find a romantic partner who measured up to him. Maybe such efforts always carry a hint of doom; as a firebrand who sought both to imitate her dad and defy him, I was bound to get equivocal results. Caroline too had been beholden to the commanding presence of her psychoanalyst father, and had been hurt in relationships with men. The exception was Morelli, who because of their separation I wouldn't meet until more than a year into our friendship. The spring of the publication of *Pack of Two*, we threw a book party in the middle of the Fells. I looked over the rise to see a soft-eyed man with a gentle demeanor approaching with a camera slung over his shoulder. When Lucille ran toward him, he got down on one knee to greet her. "Oh my God, is that Morelli?" I asked, and Caroline nodded with a familiar wistful grin—one that translated into *What do you think?* "I think you should marry him," I said, "and let him raise the kids."

My half-cocked remark held a lot of truth, and was less reckless than it sounded. Caroline had written about Morelli for years, in columns and in her memoir; even during their faux breakup, they had stayed connected in a way that most ex-partners can't or won't. So I already knew, given her history with men, that his generosity and caretaking both sustained and confused her. But I also knew that day by the way Lucille responded to him, and he to us, that Morelli was different from the men Caroline had been involved with, particularly the horrid character of Julian, the controlling lover she had portrayed in *Drinking*. We used to laugh with relief at the traps we'd avoided; in a typical incident from our parallel lives, it turned out that we'd even fled the same man years before. When the guy started describing the sunsets he planned to show me, I had rolled my eyes and broken our date; Caroline had gone out with him later that year and wound up chauffering him all over town at her expense. Our age difference, along with circumstance, had placed us on separate points along the same path. In the wake of her parents' deaths and her stopping drinking, Caroline was at the start of a whole new realm of self-reliance; like me, she had found that a dog had elicited in her a sustenance and warmth she'd never imagined. In some ways Morelli's very kindness and staying power got in the way of those discoveries—I suspect she needed him to go away for a while, but not too far, which is what he did.

WHEN I WAS IN the throes of leaving Sam, my version of Caroline's Julian, he had looked at me across the dinner table one night, mired in his own drama of defeat, and said to me, "You know, sometimes the light of you is just a little too bright." This was a charming spin on the old it's-not-you-it's-me routine, and it took me months after our breakup to sort out my wants from his finely scripted sorrows. The women's movement had given me a leg up on all kinds of rough times, and yet, to my chagrin, I'd brought few of those resources into this relationship. The shards of my fallen-heroine myth were part of the problem: Playing on a gender theme throughout history, I'd confused need with love and love with sacrifice. Finding my way out of that crevasse, onto the solid ground of my own quiet life, had been as liberating and hope-filled as stopping drinking had been five years earlier. From the outside this may have looked like a decline, or at least a retreat: In the years since I'd left Sam, I'd given up downtown dinner parties (and Sisyphean efforts at being constantly divine) for nights at home with the dog; I cared now about work, and friendships, and the white creature in my living room, and none of these assets was subject any longer to negotiation.

These life lessons—about grace and autonomy, about how to love without giving away the farm—were crystallized for me in the woods with Caroline and the dogs. If the two of us had had our trust shaken in lousy relationships, it was being rebuilt here, with tools we hadn't quite been aware we possessed. For us, dog training was a shared experience of such reward that the education was infused throughout the friendship. Much of training a dog is instinctive; it is also a complex effort of patience and observation and mutual respect. Caroline and I could spend hours discussing conditioning and the intricacies of attachment; only two women who had spent years in the revelatory light of therapy could have found such rich bounty in, say, the equivocal use of the word "no" in canine communication. We bolstered each other through miles and months of training and interpretation; what had been a private pleasure for each of us was now an on-going dialogue.

A less conscious instruction was taking place along-side the articulated one. The woman I felt myself be-coming, with Clementine beside me, appeared in part because I had something to protect. Now I understood how a woman could lift a Volkswagen off her child's foot, or all the other adrenaline-soaked stories in the culture about power and love. I was learning firsthand that nur-turance and strength were each the lesser without the other.

I had first encountered this truth during a vulnerable time in Clementine's life, when I was trying to make her submit to what is commonly known as an "alpha roll"— a questionable practice often prescribed for unruly pup-pies, in which the human rolls the pup on her back and contains her until the dog stops struggling. Most puppies will acquiesce within one or two tries; Clemen-tine, whose temperament was both dominant and gentle, was having none of it. I would roll her over and she would struggle relentlessly, then, once released, spring to her feet and bark in protest. Ever conscious of the need to establish my authority, I'd try again. The third time, in the middle of the struggle, I had a bird's-eye view of what I was doing. Crouched there on the floor, I saw my-self as my father, who had been flummoxed and enraged by his daughters' adolescence. He couldn't keep us from growing up and away, and so he yelled and threatened and tried to get us to back down, which had only made it worse.

My mother had asked me once after I was grown what my dad could have done differently, instead of bullying his way through my rebellion. "I wish he'd just told me how much he loved me," I answered her. "I wish he could have just said, 'You are precious to me; I won't let you put yourself in danger.' " This exchange came back to me in a sorrowful flash when I had my small, intractable sled dog on the floor. Did she really need to be convinced that I was in charge? I was ten times her size; I had language, consciousness, and history behind me— my species had been domesticating hers for thousands of years. I was playing master sergeant when there was no need for any standing army.

My agenda disappeared in that moment, and Clementine's burgeoning temperament was given the room it required. I let her go and hoisted her onto my shoulder, and she fell on me like a kid being carted home from the fair. From that moment on, everything changed between us. Wherever I danced, she followed.

I told Caroline this story one afternoon at the Fells when we were circling the fire trails in autumn. We were talking that day about the realized life versus the external picture of it: the assumptions and projections that we all make about other people's lives. Each of us had endured complaints from our non-dog friends about our disappearance into the woods, but what our critics couldn't see were the glorious recesses of this new place: the colors and smells and hints of sublimity that these walks ensured. Caroline, so often a captive to her own reserve, was now rolling around on the forest floor, laughing and wrestling with the dogs without a shred of inhibition. I was training Clementine off-lead, using hand signals to get her into a down-stay from ten yards away, and she would start to whimper after a few seconds, then break the stay and come charging toward me. Pack of four, we were, planting flags all over the province of our rearranged lives. So much of what we valued was being played out in those woods, in what we were building with the dogs and with each other. And so I looked at Caroline at the end of that fine day and said, "You know—after all this, I don't think that any man could ever treat me badly again."

TO PEOPLE WHO have spent their lives thick with the bounty of other people, attachment itself is complex but assumed. For the introvert, it is a more nebulous territory. I was able to be effusive and warm in my human interactions because I knew when and how they would end: end of day, end of party, end of walk, end of relationship. In the drinking years, the bourbon was the soul mate waiting on the trail, the fixed love object that made me eschew or shrug off others. But walls, whether built by brick or isolation, don't come down without a corresponding amount of labor. Without even knowing it, I think Caroline and I coaxed each other into the light. We did this slowly, and with such pronounced attention to the other's autonomy that neither of us had to move an inch to get away from the other.

I think back now to the small measures of trust gained in that first year of the friendship, the ways we went from mutual caution to inseparable ease, and so much of it now seems like a careful, even silent exchange. I knew about Caroline's history with anorexia, and on our long excursions in the woods, I would take two graham crackers out of my pocket and hand her one matter-of-factly, without even looking at her. I must have realized, half consciously, that she was too polite to refuse; we were both on the thin side, and so my offering, to the anorectic mind, was relatively unthreatening. Then I started adding small chunks of chocolate to the stash. The primal and mutual pleasure of this act touches me now, though I couldn't have articulated it, or maybe even recognized it, at the time. After years of struggling with a harsh inner voice of denial and control, Caroline was letting me feed her—reluctantly at first, then with some relief. And I, so long afraid of having anyone need me too much, was foraging around for nuts and berries, bringing them back to the creature I loved.

Counting on each other became automatic. When I found a sweater in Texas I wanted, I learned to buy two, which was easier than seeing the look of disappointment on Caroline's face when I returned home with only one. When she went out from the boathouse on a windy day, she gave me her schedule in advance, which assuaged her worst-case scenario of flipping the boat, being hit on the head by an oar, and leaving Lucille stranded at home. I still have my set of keys to her house, to locks and doors that no longer exist, and I keep them in my glove compartment, where they have been moved from one car to another in the past couple of years. Someday I will throw them in the Charles, where I lost the seat to her boat and so much else.

"WHAT ARE YOU DOING?" I would say in the early afternoon, when I called after the writing hours were done and before the walking ones began. "Waiting for you to call," she would answer, half kidding, and we would dive in: the morning papers (two each), the rowing and swimming ledger (five miles on the water, 1,500 meters in it), the twenty-four-hour chronicle of dramas and annoyances that bookend a day. When we'd gotten to the pond, after the phone call and before dusk, Caroline would link her arm into mine and say, "Sooo . . . ?" as we wound around the reservoir, starting yet another sentence in the infinite conversation. According to the old rule book, men had sports and women had talking; Caroline and I cultivated both, finding that our logging of miles on river or land enhanced the internal ground we covered. And yet I find now that writing about a friendship that flourished within the realm of connection and routine has all the components of trying to capture air. The dailiness of our alliance was both muted and essential: We were the lattice that made room for the rose.

6.

IF COMPATIBILITY IS PART LUCK AND PART LABOR, our mettle had been tested by the summer trips we took, together and apart. More than one of those vacations turned into rescue missions. She bailed me out from a miserable, rainy couple of weeks in Truro when she showed up with a tape of *The Sopranos* and a bread pudding from Formaggio. I returned the favor a month later, when she and Morelli were stranded in bad weather in New Hampshire, by sending them a tape of *Survivor*—Caroline's secret pleasure—by overnight mail. One year when she and Tom got to Chocorua a day or two ahead of me, she called me in Cambridge, begging me to come a day early. "You've got to get up here," she whispered. "The man made me go on a nine-mile hike today. I can hardly move."

God forbid Tom should learn her limitations; Caroline had nearly pinned him arm wrestling the year before. I was an easier companion, at least when it came to mountain hikes; we had also learned that we could exist on parallel tracks in silent space. Early in our friendship we had gone to a house of her family's on Gay Head on Martha's Vineyard, in late March. The landscape on that end of the island is wild even in high summer; at the start of spring, the place was cold and desolate. It was a hard trip. There were new crops of ticks in the marshes surrounding the house, and after a run the dogs would emerge from high grass looking as though they'd been sprinkled with poppy seeds. Caroline and I bundled ourselves in sweatshirts, armed with brushes and rubbing alcohol, and sat on the floor in the waning light, combing dozens of ticks off the dogs' coats. I had such a case of cabin fever after two days of rain that I drove twenty miles across island to swim in a hotel pool; Caroline spent most of the time I was gone talking to Morelli on the phone, distraught about the memories the house held. By the time we closed up the house and headed to Vineyard Haven for the ferry, we were both worn out and beyond any efforts at good cheer. An hour before departure, we drove the car into the long ferry queue that is part of Vineyard life, and got out with the dogs to hang around in the parking lot until we left.

Then on the boardwalk across the way, I saw a silhouette that sent my stomach into my throat. A man was sitting on a bench reading *The New York Times*, and I was convinced it was Sam, the man I had split up with five years earlier—whose letters I had never answered, whom I hadn't seen since that day I left him in an airport in another city. "Oh my God, Caroline," I said, "that's Sam." She knew all the stories about this piece of pain, including the fact that he spent a lot of time on the Vineyard, and she knew with one look how unhappy I was at the prospect of running into him.

"Hold the dogs," she said abruptly, giving me Lucille's leash. "Don't freak out. I know what to do." She moved too fast for me to respond, and so I stood there while she marched toward the man on the bench. She got within about ten yards to his right, and then yelled out his name—smiling and waving at a nonexistent person beyond him. She was acting on the assumption that if the man was Sam, we would know it immediately, because he would start in recognition; if I was mistaken and he ignored her, then we wouldn't have to spend the next two hours dodging ghosts from the past.

The man barely glanced her way before returning to his paper. But everyone else—well, Caroline was hollering and waving while no one was waving back, and she had an audience of sixty or seventy people staring at her. This was a woman so shy she could barely endure any kind of spotlight. But now she had made me laugh until my stomach hurt, and made a fool of herself in public to give me some peace. I had never loved her more than in that moment. She came striding back to where I stood, proud of her antics and glad to see me laughing. "That guy's about a hundred years old," she said, shrugging, and took ahold of Lucille's leash and lit a cigarette.

—

THOSE CIGARETTES. I would like to leave them out of this story but cannot. I had learned on the Vineyard trip to grant Caroline the time she needed each day for the *New York Times* crossword puzzle—a sine qua non for which, as the week progressed and the puzzles became harder, she required absolute silence. If you interrupted her focus she would shoot you a look of such withering scorn that it could stop a preacher in his tracks. My rules of togetherness were equally demanding. She could survive a three-hour car trip with me only by chewing nicotine gum; it was a testament to our immediate fondness for each other that I understood her smoking and she tolerated my aversion to it. I had quit four years earlier, and it had taken me years of wanting to quit before I was able, and so I knew that cultivating her desire to stop was far more effective than any threats or scare tactics I could throw her way.

This equanimity didn't always reign; the closer we became, the less I was able to bear her smoking. I started hollering at her on the phone one day, after I'd been pressuring her about trying to quit and she'd asked me to back off and I couldn't, and I said something that makes me ache to remember it. "You're eight years younger than I am," I cried. "I don't want to have to bury you."

I was hardly alone in my worry. Caroline's mother, before she died, had begged her to stop smoking, and Caroline told me more than once that she was no match for the coalition of her sister, Becca, and me—with the pressure from the two of us, she knew she would have to quit. But she loved smoking the way my dad had loved it, with his three-pack-a-day habit that went on for decades. I had grown up with the smell of his coffee and his Camels eliciting a feeling of safety, and I knew this attachment could be a tangle of poison and desire. Most addictions, Caroline's included, are both intricate and predictable. The ever-complicit brain turns the craving into a narrative: The cigarette or bourbon or obsessive relationship becomes the guide rope, the way we navigate the day. Caroline believed she couldn't write without a cigarette, couldn't endure a night or an hour within the vast caverns of a tobaccoless world. She tried nicotine gum and tried staring at photos of smokers' lungs; she researched in-treatment facilities for nicotine addiction. And she finally managed to stop on her own, just before she had to.

It was not a source of trouble between us, but rather of mutual distress. If Caroline and I shared some of the most idyllic times of both our lives, the core of our friendship came from the rougher excursions we endured together. From that first winter afternoon in the Harvard ball fields, "Oh no—I need you" had become an admission and a clarion call—the tenet of dependency that forms the weft of friendship. We needed each other so that we could count on the endless days of forests and flat water, but the real need was soldered by the sadder, harder moments—discord or helplessness or fear—that we dared to expose to each other.

It took me years to grasp that this grit and discomfort in any relationship are an indicator of closeness, not its opposite. We learned to fight well and fairly from the beginning: When Tom witnessed one of our straight-on conflicts, he grabbed his book and headed up the stairs. "I grew up with sisters," he said as he retreated. "I know where this is going." We had great power to hurt each other, and because we acknowledged this weapon we tried never to use it. Besides the smoking, I don't know that we ever fought about anything important. We could both be haughty and snappish and overly sensitive, and yet we forgave these traits in each other almost immediately and without much of a struggle.

Our trust allowed for a shorthand that let us get to the point quickly. Caroline knew that when I headed toward my basement corner of worldview melancholia, it manifested itself in ways both comic and treatable. For years a lovely young Guatemalan woman cleaned my house every couple of weeks. She adored Clementine and would regularly say, "Ooh, someday I'm just going to take her with me!" One afternoon after Lilian had left, when I was feeling assaulted by life's little treacheries, I became convinced that she was serious. In a fit of maternal anxiety, I called Caroline, who knew Lilian and her sweet, teasing spirit. "Do you think she meant it?" I asked. "I mean, really, do you think she might take her?" Caroline was kind that day—she neither laughed nor scoffed—but for years afterward, whenever I would start to go off-kilter about the world and its potential evils, all Caroline had to do for a reality check was say, with diagnostic calm, "I'm afraid Lilian is stealing the dog again."

These were the day-to-day dramas we confessed to each other and lessened by their expression alone. Caroline would call fretting about a potluck dinner; she was so shy, she dreaded it for days. I told her to make an appearance and duck out early; she managed to stay for eleven minutes. She speeded me up when I dawdled, and I consoled her when her hyperefficiency got her into trouble, as when she plowed ahead into a parking garage and almost took the boat rack off her car. We divided the world up into separate strengths: I was good with computers and veterinary tasks; Caroline was in charge of home repair and any feat requiring physical strength. When it came to matters of the soul and psyche, we each knew how to tend to the other. But Caroline's range of acceptance was larger than mine, and so were her skills of diplomacy.

PRIVATELY, AND NOT altogether in jest, we believed that all people could be consigned to dog breeds. "God, he is *such* an apricot poodle," Caroline would say about someone vain or entitled, or, between her teeth, about a woman who brayed: *"Beagle."* Morelli listened to us doing this during a walk one afternoon and stopped in his tracks; he had gone from amused to incredulous: "You guys are really serious about this, aren't you?" This taxonomy became a code for human personality, and whenever anyone would wander onto our field of attention, the inevitable question became which breed he or she might be. We enjoyed making Morelli a chocolate Lab (great heart, sense of humor) and I insisted Caroline was a collie (smart, high-strung, loyal), but for years we pondered where I belonged. Finally one day at the beginning of a walk she declared her research over.

"I've decided what breed you are," she said with dry certainty. I swallowed; this was important stuff. She paused before giving me the verdict: "A young female German shepherd dog."

"Oh—but . . ." I was flustered and a little unnerved. "I mean, they're really great dogs," I said, "and I know they're smart and everything. But they're so *serious*. And they're herders—they're so bossy, they run every other dog into the ground."

Her smile was her answer. "Well, that's why I made you a young female," she said. "To soften it a little."

7

THE COMPETITION WE FOSTERED, ALONE AND TO-
gether, became a pleasure rather than a hindrance: We
brought our rivalry into the light and tried to tame it.
Every time I swam, I chose a lane near an unwitting op-
ponent, preferably a man, who was faster than I; then I
flung myself through my laps for the next half hour, trying to catch him. Each October after the world-class
Head of the Charles regatta, Caroline would go out on
the water alone and row the three-plus-mile course, timing herself to see where she fell in her age and weight
group. The race itself was too nerve-racking for her, and
she didn't care about competing publicly. Like me, she
set an anonymous golden mean and raced against it.

Caroline always said that she and her sister had navigated their shared terrain by divvying up the goods.
"Becca got math and science, I got English and history,"
she liked to say, and we did something similar with our
curriculum in the writing life: Our sublimation within

the safer realm of athletics allowed us to bolster each other professionally. According to our unspoken rule, Caroline was the columnist and I was the critic; she wrote about the personal and psychological, while I claimed the province of analysis and interpretation. It helped that I was older, and that we both loved our work and had been rewarded in kind. I think we were each good enough at what we did that we could applaud, mostly unequivocally, the other's victories.

When one of us was the clear superior, it softened the odds—it took the pressure off the other's Inner Marine. You will *always* be the better rower, I told her one summer, with relief; that meant I could actually relax and let her train me. And rowing was the shared Eden that allowed us unbridled effort and victory, whatever the race. Caroline's willowy prowess on the water testified to years of work, and she took unabashed pride in this accomplishment: One of life's grace notes had been the morning when Harry Parker, legendary oarsman and Harvard crew coach, spotted Caroline on the river and gave her a thumbs-up in front of his amateur eights, then had her demonstrate her stroke. In winter, desolate at the long season when the river was frozen, Caroline retired to the gym, where she had been known to do stomach crunches with a ten-pound weight on her chest. Weaker but only slightly less fanatical, I nearly killed myself trying to do the plough (a contortionist's back stretch) on my kitchen floor, simply because Caroline had shown it to me that afternoon on the asphalt path at Fresh Pond. In the off-season, I joined Gold's Gym, listening to the male weight lifters make primate noises while I suffered through a half hour on the indoor rowing machines. Walking the icy trails of January, we fantasized about winter-sport possibilities: Was it too late in life to take up the luge? By the time New England's erratic spring arrived, we were pawing the ground like crazed horses. We knew that thrashing around on the water during a cold and windy March could be frustrating and even foolish.

But within a year after that first summer at Chocorua, where Caroline had shown me the fire, I also knew there was no such thing as a bad row. It opened up the world in such powerful and quotidian ways that the promise of it, whether in February or August, gave us a calendar by which to mark our passion. From my first full season on the water, Caroline indulged my fervor with fond recognition of what she had been through years before. If the water was perfect—glassy and still—we would drop anything (dentist appointments, dinner obligations) to get on the river. I often went out in early evening, when the wildlife had settled and the shoreline had gone from harsh brightness to Monet's gloaming, and then I would row back to the dock in golden light, the other scullers moving like fireflies across the water.

My stubbornness and upper-body strength compensated for my weak leg, and within a couple of seasons I had managed a passable stroke. I got stronger, faster, exhilarated on a daily basis. I went out in wind gusts and rain and came back spent and calm. Caroline had warned me that my entire relationship to the river would change, and to be careful driving—with the Charles River winding alongside Memorial Drive, it was easy to forget about oncoming traffic if you were rubbernecking the condition of the water. "The river will become a character in your life," Caroline told me. "You'll be amazed how much influence it will have on your day."

By autumn, I had mapped out an entire country of flora and fauna, much of it invisible from land. I began to set my internal clock of miles logged by the landmarks I encountered. There was the man who played bagpipes each morning on a bend in the river—"The Halls of Montezuma" and, if I was lucky, "Amazing Grace"—and the muskrat a quarter mile upstream, appearing with such reliability that I could believe it was for my benefit. (There was also, less decorous, the exhibitionist on the wooded end of the river who flashed women rowers, about whom Caroline had warned me.) Most of all there was the arc and geography of the river and my place upon it. By September the goslings of spring would be learning to dive on their own; the marshes had turned from green to golden rose. All of it offered a palette in time and space where beauty was anchored to change.

I usually saw Caroline on her way upriver: the blond ponytail, the back of a dancer, a stroke as fluid as it was exact. (She never saw me until I called out to her, and even then she had to squint. The glasses she needed and refused to wear never left the glove box of her car.) Some days we would meet on a wide stretch by the finish line of the Head of the Charles. The moment she squared her blades and stopped, Caroline checked her watch, sometimes surreptitiously; even on the gentlest of rows, she was gauging her time. Then she would watch my stroke and give me a drill to occupy me for a few days. "Use your abs for the recovery," she would say. "Stop checking behind you; you're clear. Use your thumbs before you feather!" I thrilled to the language as well as the instruction.

In the summer of 2000, when I was forty-nine and Caroline was about to turn forty-one, we decided that we had one last chance to realize a dream: to row in a double in our age division in the Head of the Charles. We were mistaken about the age stipulation, which accepts any pairing with an age average over forty, but the fantasy stuck, and it gave us a mission for the season. It was the sort of goal we both loved, one that we could discuss endlessly while incorporating its training demands into our daily routines. Because we both fell into the under-130-pound weight division, we decided that we would bill ourselves as the Literary Lightweights—good for a few laughs on the river, we thought, and maybe even a corporate sponsor or two. Morelli, who had long wanted Caroline to show her stuff in a race, had T-shirts made for us with a tiny oarsman on the breast; he promised to hang off the bridges and photograph us during training sessions. As the more accomplished rower, Caroline would steer while I rowed stroke, which meant that she would have to slow her pace to mine.

This handicap was of no consequence to her and mattered greatly to me. I added stomach crunches and leg lifts to my regimen, and started taking my pulse after sprints on the water. I plied Caroline with progress reports: stroke rate, heart rate, technical or psychic breakthroughs. She endured my single-mindedness and placated me when she could. "I'm afraid I'll fail you," I said one day, with great seriousness; my German shepherd spirit at the ready, I had already turned a lark into a challenge of enormous weight.

"I will *only* do this with you if it can be fun," she told me, and my antennae went up. "Fun" was a nebulous concept for both of us; her therapist was always trying to impose it on her. Fun was far more difficult to get a handle on than zeal. But I listened to her that day and tried to bank my fires, and eventually my training rituals became an end unto themselves.

We missed the entrance for our division that year, which for first-timers is decided by lottery. I think we were both relieved, for two reasons. One was that we had started training late in the season and weren't ready to race. The other, more revealing reason was that Caroline and I were each so goal-oriented—she once told me that "mastery" was her favorite feeling—that we wanted the next season, and the next, to have an occasion to set our hopes and focus toward. Like most odysseys, ours on the Charles was more about the journey than the finish line. The metaphor of rowing may have been what we loved the most: the anticipation, the muscles spent and miles logged, the September harvest moon. Because we both possessed that single trait that makes a lifelong rower— endurance—we declared that we would row the Head together in our seventies, when the field had thinned sufficiently to give us a fighting chance. The fantasy would fuel us for two more winters.

After the 2000 regatta had come and gone, in late October, we took out the double to see how we might have measured up. It was a fiasco from the start: The boat had been rigged for giants, which meant that we were half prostrate during a full stroke; we didn't realize this mechanical mishap until we were too far out on the water to make adjustments. The wind picked up, accompanied by haphazard gusts that made the river a sea of chop. Then the rain started—a cold autumn rain that pelted us from behind and threatened our nerves as well as our grip on the oars. Caroline responded to these horrid conditions by rowing harder. My stroke grew ragged and then uneven, until she finally told me to stop rowing altogether; if my rhythm was too far off, she would be battling against me. Frustrated by my own performance, I was in awe of hers: The worse the rain and the stronger the current, the steadier she became. We rowed the entire course, cheering as we crossed a deserted finish line. We were soaked from rain and waves, elated from laughter and exertion. I lay back in the boat and let Brutita row us home.

8.

THAT DECEMBER, A BLIZZARD STRANDED ME FOR days in Texas, where I had gone to see my family for the holidays. I finally managed to get on a flight that was rerouted through Chicago to Massachusetts. Caroline, in touch by phone during the ordeal, had taken Clementine to my apartment an hour before my flight was scheduled to arrive in Boston. At the end of a marathon travel day, I sank into the back of a cab at Logan Airport, wanting nothing more than to be in my own home, wanting my couch and the feel of Clementine's ruff and the sound of Caroline's voice on the phone. "Hostage to attachment," I remember thinking, the words coming out of nowhere. Leaving town was what told me, reminded me, how much I relied on these two creatures to give purchase to the emotional ground of my life. If by now this realization was more consoling than unnerving, it was still a radical departure from my norm. However skittish Caroline could be, I may have been worse—more stubborn, more reflexively prideful—when the real bruisers of life showed up. In crisis, I circled my wagons, more afraid of being disappointed by someone than of going it alone.

For reasons that probably have to do with temperament and heritage both, I had spent a lifetime cultivating a little too much independence. Absurd or commendable, a lot of this behavior was unnecessarily severe. I'd hitchhiked long distances alone in my twenties; for years I'd swum the Wellfleet ponds after Labor Day, when they were deserted, until an early autumn thunderstorm convinced me this was a bad idea. Such feats, I privately held, were heroic in correlation to the amount of suffering invoked. Even after I stopped drinking, I never wanted my solitude to limit my range, so I signed up for work assignments that took me to Wyoming or London or anywhere I hadn't been—gritting my teeth at the difficulty of such pursuits, plowing ahead because I thought I should be willing to bear the pain and isolation in order to glean the adventure.

But as much as I complained about my solitude, I also required it. I put a high price on my freedom from obligation, of having to report to no one. My sister, contentedly married a thousand miles away, laughed whenever I expressed the fantasy of holding out to find the right man to marry. "I don't know, Caldwell," she would say, resorting to our old adolescent habit of using surnames for each other. "I don't think you could do it. You'd need a pretty long leash."

The truth was that I had always fled. The men I didn't marry; the relationships I had walked away from or only halfheartedly engaged in—there were always well-lit exits, according to building code, in every edifice I helped create. "Let's face it," a male friend, single and in his forties, said to me one day about our unpartnered status. "Neither one of us got here without a lot of fancy footwork." I laughed at the time, but I was unsettled by how astute the comment was, and more obvious to him than to me.

AFTER THE CAB HAD dropped me at my apartment that winter night, I hugged the dog and called Caroline's answering machine, to let her know I had made it. It was after eight p.m. and I didn't really expect to talk with her. "I'm home, I'm all right," I said. "Don't bother picking up. I'm heading to the store—I'll talk to you tomorrow."

Twenty minutes later, I was loading groceries into my old Volvo when an out-of-control driver came veering through the parking lot at high speed and plowed into the back of my car. It happened so fast that I later remembered only a blur of white movement, then flying through the air. The Volvo had taken a bullet for me: The impact of one car into another had sent me flying like a billiard ball. When I came to, I was on my hands and knees on the pavement, yards away from point of impact; I had blood spewing from my chin and I was cursing. A group of people were standing around me. Somebody called 911; another disembodied voice claimed to recognize me, and gathered what was left of the spilled groceries to take to my house. When the EMTs arrived and strapped me to a backboard, I started arguing with them about cutting off my jeans and Lucchese boots. By the time I got to the hospital, I was giddy with adrenaline and telling jokes: that false pride of the trenches.

I was on the backboard for an hour waiting for an X-ray; by the time they released me, it was eleven p.m. My injuries were not serious—stitches in my chin, sprains and contusions but no broken bones—but I hollered in pain when I tried to put weight on my leg. Overwhelmed by more dire emergencies, the hospital staff gave me a cane and called me a cab. In the three hours I had been there, never once did it occur to me, with a phone four feet away from where I lay, to call Caroline or anyone else for help.

Or I should say that when it did occur to me, I dismissed it with the defensive sangfroid of crisis. It was Sunday night; I knew Morelli would be at Caroline's, spending the night. I didn't want to wake them, and I knew if I called they would feel duty-bound to come to the hospital. Pleased by my self-reliance, I half stumbled, half crawled up the stairs to my apartment.

But when I got inside, when I was in my living room at midnight, with Clementine nosing my bloodstained jeans, I broke down. I had phoned my parents back in

Texas, who were expecting word that my plane had arrived safely, and lied through my teeth. They were in their eighties, my dad was in the first stage of Alzheimer's, and I saw no need to alarm them. Then all my derring-do collapsed and I dialed Caroline's number. My voice broke when she answered. "I'm all right, I'm all right," I kept saying, an insistent preface to the story so I wouldn't scare her. We stayed on the phone until she had convinced me to find something to eat and get into bed.

My car, a ten-year-old Volvo, had been totaled. The next day, Caroline came to get me and we drove back to the store parking lot; she went inside the market to grab some essentials for me while I tried to start the car and get the registration. Ten minutes later, she came out to find me standing, glazed-eyed, near the place where I'd landed; there was a pool of dried blood on the asphalt. On the drive home she was unnervingly quiet, and finally she blurted out the reason. "I keep thinking that if I had just picked up the phone when you first called," she said, "this never would have happened. Three minutes later, and you'd have been out of the path of that car."

I knew this inner dialogue of self-blame; it was treacherous and unwinnable. Caroline was worried not just that she'd failed to intervene with the stupid calamities of fate, but that she was somehow responsible—that her isolationist tendencies had put me in harm's way. This was the sort of mind-set we could both engage in, and so I postulated the opposite: If she *had* picked up, I insisted, I might well have been just walking out of the store, and in the car's direct line of fire.

For all the gritty education this incident provided, its one indelible moment, there long after the bruises were healed and the car replaced, was the one I had told Caroline about that afternoon: the thought that went through my mind when I was midair. The world appears with ferocious technicolor during crisis, and a decade later, I remember the visual arc of my body being airborne, my sight line about two feet higher than normal. But what I remember most was the territorial assault I felt, the indignation, while I was sailing through space. *How dare you,* the body and mind felt in furious accord. *I'm in the middle of a life here.* I was outraged because I had been working on this story line for years, and I knew it was not yet finished.

...

AFTER I HAD LIVED IN THE EAST FOR A DECADE, long enough to winnow the realities from the dreams, I was driving down Brattle Street one winter night at the start of a storm, when the snow was surfing the currents of a soft wind, and I had the dissonant thought that I could grow old here—something I had never thought about anywhere before, and certainly not during a New England winter. But Cambridge had reached out to me from the beginning. I loved the ornery brick-lined sidewalks and self-contained serenity that the town projected: all that formidable history bumping into pear blossoms and street musicians.

I had danced around the idea of owning property for years, usually as an alternate reality to wherever I was. I fantasized about a little piece of land in Truro, on the then desolate end of Cape Cod. I thought about a small house in Austin where I could spend winters, or a farmhouse outside the city with room for a couple of dogs. As the search had grown more realistic, I began looking at houses all over Greater Boston, exhausting myself with possibilities or mooning over properties I couldn't afford. I was like a wolf circling its parameters, looking everywhere but the epicenter of my life.

The false starts probably mirrored my tendency toward flight and longing. Leave Texas, then miss it forever. Love your family from two thousand miles away. Refuse to marry, then spend your life complaining that you should have. The ingrained trait that my mother had called brooding had a free run when it came to where I imagined I belonged. I could explore alternate universes to my heart's content within the world of geographical could-have-beens, where the endings were always kinder and the real estate cheaper. "I should have stayed in the Panhandle, and I'd be happily married to some rancher and have five or six kids," I once announced to my therapist, who typically did not laugh out loud at such pronouncements. "I think the operative word here is 'happily,'" he said, always ready to scorch an illusion when he could. As a follow-up joke he sent me a map of the actual town of Happy, Texas, a little place of about seven hundred people south of Amarillo. I kept the map of Happy on my study wall for years, to remind me of the Elysian Fields we all envision.

"SCRATCH A FANTASY and you'll find a nightmare." This was one of Caroline's favorite sayings, spoken originally in regard to a mutual friend, a woman who had chased a dream life abroad and wound up trapped and unhappy. Then the saying became code for all those seemingly perfect lives being lived someplace else, with better jobs or partners or inner states. Whenever I would say (in winter or traffic, or on a bad day), "Why do we live here?" Caroline would respond, instantly, "Fresh Pond and Starbucks." Starbucks wasn't yet on every corner in America, but Caroline was shorthanding for the ineffable whole: the surly poet on the corner, or the river at dusk, or the store with the butcher who knew us by name. We lived here for each other, and for everyone else we loved within twenty miles, and for all the good reasons people live where they live. They need the view of a wheat field or an ocean; they need the smell of a thunderstorm or the sound of a city. Or they need to leave, so that they can invent what they need someplace else.

According to our mutually mythic pasts, I was the exile and Caroline the child who had stayed. I'd fled the bleak farm and ranchlands of the Panhandle, made it to Austin five hundred miles south, and lived in San Francisco for a couple of years before finally heading for the East. Caroline had grown up in Cambridge, a few blocks from the Radcliffe quad; when she left for college, she went to Brown University in Providence, an hour away. She came back to Cambridge four years later and had strayed only so far as a couple of neighborhoods from her childhood home. Her familiar was my exotic—her Cambridge was my Amarillo—and it seemed part of the price of urbanity, like growing up in Greenwich Village, that it was too cool a hometown to flee. The year after her parents' deaths, Caroline had bought an attached Victorian house in the middle of Cambridge, with wide pine floors and an exposed brick chimney and ten-foot ceilings. More than a century old, the place was all angles and elegance, with comfortable mission furniture and Lucille's toys within carefully organized reach. I lived a few miles away, in a light-filled second-floor apartment I had rented for a decade. Much of the ambivalence I felt about setting down roots was softened by the sense of shelter I knew Caroline's house provided her. When pragmatism finally won out over inertia, I began the Sunday open house slog through scores of property listings—the standard heart-of-darkness journey that accompanies house hunting. And Caroline, intrepid soldier, went along for the entire march.

Financial limitations aside, a property search for a single woman can be a nerve-racking expedition, complete with blueprints of the status quo. I found that residential real estate, particularly in New England, was an illustration of demographics: Single-family houses were just that, colonials and Victorians built with nuclear families in mind. Every time I visited one, my stomach sank and I felt an overwhelming fatigue. Formal dining rooms, upstairs bedrooms? I wanted to weep from estrangement. The architecture-for-singles had its own problems, diminutive spaces and features that seemed a subtle punishment for going it alone. There were oppressively small houses with low ceilings and cramped rooms. Or apartments in old three-deckers or large apartment buildings, which meant you gave up a yard and privacy and parking for an affordable mortgage.

Caroline and I dissected every angle of this morass. I would drive home from Sunday open houses, spent and empty-headed, and call her for a reality check, or she would meet me at the appointed place and march through the rooms, cheerful and skeptical at once. Did I really want to live in this gorgeous third-floor aviary, she would ask, with my bum leg and a sixty-pound dog? It was the season of bidding wars and land rushes, and places were selling in a day or an hour—one manic agent had called me at nine-thirty at night, wanting me to bid on a place I hadn't even seen. I'd been in this queue of desperation (and lost) a couple of times, only to be outbid by those with more money or less sangfroid than I.

The high stakes of real estate hunting fed my anxiety; the market in those days was like a game of musical chairs, with everyone frantically trying to get situated before the music died.

In early spring of 2001, I made an offer on a little house in the suburbs with a large, overgrown yard; Caroline had climbed up the back fence the day before the open house to get a look at it. Then I panicked at the last minute. I saw my future unfolding before me with years of manicured streets and quiet New England reserve, and the picture horrified me. As nebulous as they may have seemed from the outside, my criteria had been honed by years of considering what I *didn't* want—and by the outlines of what my spirit craved. What I wanted was a dorm for grown-ups, someplace with flowers and dogs and people who looked like I felt. A colleague had articulated this netherland of intuition for me. She was a young, hip African American lesbian with a couple of body piercings, and we had talked endlessly about the perils of real estate for single women and about where we each belonged. "Let me put it this way," she said. "On the day I move in, I don't want to be the most interesting thing happening in the neighborhood." Her wry acumen came back to me the day I signed an offer on the house in the suburbs. The well-appointed agent shook my hand and said, "You seem so *interesting*!" Two days later, I took my interesting self out of the deal.

And then, on a blossom-drenched day in May when I

had nearly given up, I saw a listing for half of a rambling 1920s clapboard house on a magnolia-lined street in Cambridge. The apartment was smaller than what I wanted; the owner had painted the walls mustard yellow and hung red velvet drapes in the dining room. I cared about none of this. What had seized my heart before I ever went inside were the towering maples overlooking the long driveway, leading to an enclosed garden of dogwood and lilacs and a sixty-foot sycamore maple in the middle of the city. I had lived in New England for two decades, but I was still a Texan, and I knew the land mattered more than what was on it. I went after the trees.

Caroline loved this house. She saw past its imperfections—the lack of a guest room, the upstairs neighbor—to her certainty that it was my home. The place was halfway between the river where I rowed and the woods where we walked; the neighborhood had a park and an Italian take-out joint and a dozen people I knew. The open house lasted one hour, and at the end of the evening there were four offers on the place. A couple outbid me, outlandishly, by tens of thousands of dollars over the asking price; presumably, they had loved the trees as well. Within forty-eight hours, they withdrew their offer, and the agent called to say the place was mine if I wanted it. I told him I needed an hour to think, hung up, and called Caroline. "Yes," she said, unequivocally. *"Yes."*

Several weeks later, after the usual steep education in property buying, I was standing on the front porch of what was now my house, fiddling with the keys, dumb with fatigue and vague apprehension. Inside lay a near gut job of months of renovation. I heard someone drive up behind me and turned to see Caroline and Morelli at the curb in Caroline's Toyota RAV, both of them grinning and waving at me to wait up. I got the door unlocked just as Caroline vaulted up the front steps. And while Morelli held on to the dogs and laughed, she picked me up—I outweighed her by ten pounds—and hoisted me, like a sack of grain, over the threshold.

BY THE END of that summer, Caroline and I had become accustomed to the new routes of our conjoined paths. The apartment was a couple of blocks from Fresh Pond, and carpenters and painters were working throughout the summer. Each day I would say to Clementine, "Would you like to go to Cambridge?" and she would bark in happy reply, more at my inflection than anything else. Then we would drive to the job site, talk to the guys working inside, and head over to the reservoir to meet Caroline and Lucille at the bottom of the hill. I usually had a collection of paint chips stuffed in my back pocket. Because Samoyeds are a mix of cream and off-white, we would line up the paint chips across Clementine's back for our consideration. I had taught her the command to be still, and so she would allow this folly, standing patiently while we envisioned her coat color as, say, a trim for the dining room. One evening a woman walked past us at the duck pond, where Caroline and I stood peering at eight shades of peach, and the woman raised an eyebrow and called out, "What are you *doing* to that dog?" It was an easy summer, full of aimless walks and evening rows, and the unfolding clarity that I had taken a huge leap forward and was moving, heart and soul and cartons of books, to where I belonged.

THE MORNING OF September 11, I awoke to two voices simultaneously: the BBC announcer on the radio, reporting that the first plane had hit the World Trade Center, and my friend Pete on my answering machine, saying, "By now you probably know what's happened." The next ten minutes were the chaos of comprehension. With the TV and NPR in the background, I went online and saw that I had a three-word e-mail, still unknowing, from Caroline, sent a few minutes earlier: "did you row?" I shot one back: "New York towers hit by terrorists go downstairs and turn on TV." Caroline's office was the third-floor attic of her house, and she was usually at her desk by eight-thirty or so, cloistered from the radio and phone. Within a few minutes we were on the phone together, watching the recurring horror on the TV screen, in the same limbo as everyone else. Because the planes had originated out of Logan Airport, in Boston, there was another layer of trepidation about the city itself;

most of the land-phone and cell lines were jammed for part of the morning. Caroline and I kept getting disconnected, and finally we made a backup plan in case the infrastructure failed. If things got worse—if something happened in Boston—we would both find a way to get to Fresh Pond, which was equidistant from each of our houses; we knew we could find each other there.

It was a nonsensical plan, like millions of others made that day. We laughed about it later—the cold, anguished laugh, like combat humor, that accompanied the next few days—and considered our own bad planning: Fresh Pond wasn't exactly a Red Cross evacuation center. But now the plan's absurdity is what touches me. We were acting out of instinct, like horses headed to the barn or birds being flushed out of a tree. We were simply aiming for shelter, for our own high ground.

I wound up going for a row late that day. I didn't know what else to do. The city by midafternoon was quieter than I hope it ever is again: no planes overhead, most foot and automobile traffic suspended. Already there was the dissonance that would unfold over the next few weeks: I saw a fool on the river who called out to me, "Beautiful day, isn't it?" The whole picture-perfect scene was like the opening pastoral shot in a horror movie, except that the horror had already happened. I kept thinking about the last scenes from *On the Beach*, when the postnuclear blankness of an Australian beach is attended by the strains of "Waltzing Matilda." I was rowing under that now infamously blue sky, its emptiness chilling and inert, and I heard the eerie melancholy of "Waltzing Matilda" the entire way.

I MOVED INTO my house in early November, on Caroline's birthday. I sent her flowers that morning; she was taking care of Clementine while I watched movers run up and down the stairs. The New England fall, breathtaking and rueful under normal circumstances, had been eclipsed and upended by history's fallout. There was the suicide down the street, a woman whose fiancé had been killed in the towers. The friend of a friend whose whereabouts had never been determined. Everyone had a dozen stories like these, all the concentric circles of calamity, sad details packed in between trauma and loss. In the first few days after the attack, responding to a citywide plan, Caroline and I had stood on our porches one evening with candles held high, on the phone together; neither of us could see anyone else's glow, and this made us feel alternately weary and aghast at our futility. In the next several weeks we each stumbled into a version of survivor guilt, the flinch of awareness that could hit you in the midst of some mindless form of denial. Caroline would be playing computer solitaire and be overcome with sorrow or anxiety; I would be worrying over a renovation one minute and ready to fire all the painters the next, thinking I would send my leftover house budget to the New York firefighters fund. Everyone was getting a crash course in irony, the lesson that the grievous and the mundane exist in parallel spheres. One day I told her I felt ashamed for thinking about my house with the world in tatters, and she put her hand on my shoulder and gave a small shrug. "Paint chips . . . Osama bin Laden," she said, using her hands to plot the entire range of human experience. "This is what life turns out to be." We were all living those days inside Auden's vision of Icarus. Even with a boy falling from the sky, the ships sailed calmly on.

IT'S TAKEN YEARS FOR ME TO UNDERSTAND THAT dying doesn't end the story; it transforms it. Edits, rewrites, the blur and epiphany of one-way dialogue. Most of us wander in and out of one another's lives until not death, but distance, does us part—time and space and the heart's weariness are the blander executioners of human connection.

I have several recurring dreams about Caroline. In one she is living calmly in the woods in a little house of blues and greens; in another, I am typing a letter to her, and the ink keeps disappearing on the page as I write. She is always dead or dying in these dreams, but they are not awful, or anguished—the reach between us always trumps the loss. And yet my one unbearable dream is the one in which she is sick and in treatment and I cannot find her. We have lost touch, or a phone has been disconnected, or my key breaks off in a locked door with her on the other side. There are many variations on this dream, the one from which I wake up clawing at space, but the message is unchanged: Life, not death, has intervened.

"The holiness of the Heart's affections," Keats wrote,

trusting in nothing but that and the imagination, and I think now that Caroline and I stilled something in each other, letting us go out and engage in the larger world. And as certain as I am about fact and memory and the influence of each upon the other, finding the threads of all these stories has sent me into an eerie, detached insistence that she not yet be gone. I have all the detritus of life and death that argues the contrary: the potato au gratin recipe in her small, careful handwriting that falls out of a cookbook; a first edition of J. R. Ackerley's *My Dog Tulip* that she tracked down for me one Christmas. And a mysterious CD I found in her house after she was dead, entitled "Music for Caroline," its every song, from Norah Jones and Fiona Apple to Edith Piaf, a testament to the unknowable passions we all carry within.

Once she referred to the core ambiguities of life as "the dark side of joy," and here, these days, has been the reverse: a happy limbo in which I have brought her along on the journey. The writer's self-imposed fugue state. She has been thoroughly alive in the meadows and woods with the dogs, through each rowing lesson and argument and carefree phone call. Her death these days is somewhere down the hall, behind a closed but unlocked door. But for now she is river-tan and laughing, and pretty soon the phone will ring and one of us will say *What are you doing?* and it will all begin again.

9.

CAROLINE STARTED COUGHING IN THE WINTER. A dry cough, not yet worrisome, what seemed like a gravelly smoker's accompaniment to her singular voice. She was run down from finishing a book; she could have stood to gain ten pounds. For Christmas she gave me a mezuzah to hang near my entry door for blessings on the new house. We went out to dinner to celebrate my birthday on a frigid night in January, and she seemed subdued, but we both attributed this to work and emotional fatigue. If she was worried about her health—and she was, as it turned out—she told no one but her sister, Becca.

Two seemingly disparate incidents would later reassert themselves. Caroline tried to swim her usual forty or fifty lengths in the pool and finished only seven before she could go no farther. And then one cold, sunny afternoon in early March, her legs went out from under her at Fresh Pond with no warning. She recovered almost immediately, and sat down on a park bench to call me, minimizing the event even as she described it. For reasons I can only guess at, I absorbed this information with an urgency and dread that were disproportionate to the thing itself. I grabbed my car keys and flew out of the house, driving the few blocks to the pond to save time. When I saw her on the rise above the parking lot, I went running; by the time I reached her, she was shaking her head that it had been nothing—a momentary collapse, low blood sugar, something transient and benign.

Much of my alarm that day came from the fact that Caroline was one of the most stoic people I had ever known. She rarely got sick; when she did, she barely complained. But the coughing, hollow and persistent, didn't get better. She cut her smoking by half, then half again. Oddly, I was worried about my own health at the time. Felled by a couple of common winter bugs, I had responded, uncharacteristically, with a dark unease I couldn't shake.

Caroline had a chest X-ray and was treated for pneumonia, and the antibiotics bought her a few weeks of ease. At the end of March, on an unseasonably warm day when the river was still, we both took the boats out for the first time since the fall. She rowed her standard five miles. She would be in the hospital not long thereafter, but then, on that day, there was no wind and the water was glass. When we walked together at the end of the afternoon, she said it was the only time in fifteen years that the first row of the season had felt effortless.

That word kept coming back to me in the brutal revisionism of the days that followed. Two weeks after that perfect row, Morelli took Caroline to the emergency room late one Sunday night; she was burning up with fever and had pneumonia again. For a couple of days the doctors thought she might have tuberculosis, and we all had to wear masks in the hospital room. Those masks: She told me that she knew the news was bad when the nurses stopped wearing them, and began treating her with excruciating kindness.

I was there by chance when the doctor finished the bronchoscopy, a procedure that revealed an inoperable tumor on the lung, classified as stage-four non-small-cell adenocarcinoma. I had been absurdly positive in the two days before the procedure, consoling Caroline that she was too young to have cancer, that the mysterious spots on her liver they had detected would turn out to be nothing. Becca, who shared Caroline's poise and stillness under pressure, told me as we waited in the surgical recovery room that we should prepare for the worst, and I was stunned: She was a physician, and I trusted her far more than I did my own desperate optimism. Then the pulmonary specialist walked through the doors, threw his lanky body in a nearby chair, shrugged with a shred of kindness, and said those words that made the surrounding comments disappear: "inoperable," "necrotic," "palliative." And the obscene euphemism that telegraphs the end: "We can make her more comfortable."

I remember two things from the rest of that day with glaring clarity. One was Caroline crying as I wrapped my arms around her, after they had brought her back up to her room, when the first thing she said to me was "Are you mad at me?" It was the voice of early terror, a primal response to bad news, and to this day I don't know whether she meant because we had fought about the smoking or because she knew she was going to leave.

The other picture is from late that afternoon, after I had left the hospital long enough to walk Clementine and get some things Caroline needed. I was walking down my street toward the neighborhood park, and I saw a friend and her seven-year-old daughter up ahead on the basketball court. I looked their way just as Sophie aimed the ball and made the shot. "Mom!" she cried out. "Did you *see*?" It was her first triumph on the court, and I had been her serendipitous witness, and the force of that simple reach toward joy took my breath away. The afternoon was flush with light, and Caroline was dying, and Sophie had scored. *Mom!* There she was, the life everlasting, shooting hoops.

THE NEXT FEW DAYS were a blur of bad dispatches. More tests revealed that the cancer had metastasized to Caroline's liver and brain; by the weekend, an oncologist had joined the team, and they had started emergency radiation to the brain and a five-hour initial (and desperate) round of chemotherapy. The antibiotics had cleared up the secondary pneumonia, and there was a small window between the diagnosis and the debilitating effects of the treatment when Caroline didn't feel sick. We were all in shock, consumed with the errands of crisis, making lists of people to call and objects to procure that seemed essential: a favorite T-shirt, a tortoiseshell comb. Morelli had figured out a way to smuggle Lucille into the hospital after the evening shift had begun, and we would climb on the bed with the dog and pass around Italian takeout. Caroline started telling dumb jokes one night, with me and Morelli laughing, and then she stopped midsentence and we all stared at one another, the scene out of some weeper made-for-TV movie. Everything about it felt absurd and precious, filtered through that brief brightness that appears when death is in the room. The first night of the diagnosis, Caroline had told me that she had asked Morelli to marry her, and that we had a wedding to plan, and there was a piercing tenderness to those initial days that helped to contain the next several weeks.

She called me early one morning and I grabbed the phone and said, "Are you all right?" and she said, "Yes, I've run away—I'm thinking of going for a row." The hospital was by the river, and her upstairs room overlooked the bend of the Charles where rowers passed each morning, and she could see them at first light from her bed. Within a few days she had asked the nurses to keep the curtains closed. But on that morning she was still kidding around, still able to pretend that she would be back out there soon enough. "I miss *us*," she told me on the phone that morning. "I miss our lives together."

Because we knew everything had changed, the ways in which we communicated this to each other were as careful as they were certain. We talked about the will she was having drawn up; she told Morelli and me one night that we had to promise to walk the dogs together once a week forever. "My boat and my linen," she said, about her bequest to me; earlier that month, I had borrowed half the jackets in her closet for a trip I had to take to Austin in a few weeks. Her wryness prevailed above all else. "Oh God," she said to me the second night after the diagnosis, when we were making lists of people to call. "Now I'm going to have to listen to people's remission stories."

But at night, when I had left the hospital, I would come home and stand in the dark in the backyard, where the viburnum was in bloom, and bury my face in its fragrance and weep. After I had walked Clementine, I would go online and read about non-small-cell adenocarcinoma in the medical journals. The word "prognosis" had not yet entered our conversation, but I knew. I had called two friends who were physicians, and both had been kind enough to give me their unadorned opinion. Neither believed she had more than a few months.

I took lots of notes during these phone conversations—scrawled, elaborate notes, quotes from the doctor friends, my way of organizing the unfathomable. "Worst, most advanced," I wrote, underneath "stage four—non-small-cell adenocarcinoma." "Tumors in liver . . . Radiation will help with pain and with swelling of brain." And then, in smaller script at the end of the page: "No help at all in prolonging life."

Caroline's doctors disagreed as to the cause and origin of the tumor on the lung: A pulmonary specialist was certain it was smoking-related; an oncologist was equally sure it was not. This mattered greatly to Caroline and not at all to me, though I tried to shield her from the verdict of the lung specialist, whose work in the trenches may have steeled him from the wreckage he had to see each day. Caroline had stopped smoking in the week before the diagnosis, and she clung to this: Her recoveries from anorexia and alcoholism had been long battles against self-destruction, and she needed to know she had made one huge effort to save herself here. The reason I cared less about the tumor's origin was pragmatic: As much as I had worried about Caroline's smoking, its causative agency had not a shred of effect on the diagnosis, any more than being pushed off a building protects you from falling off it.

On Friday, the night they started the chemo, Caroline was in bed wearing the T-shirt I had brought her, an IV in her arm, when I came in. She asked if she could keep the shirt; of course, I said. She asked me to set and program her new underwater sports watch, so she could time her laps in the pool when she got out of the hospital. She had always paced her steps to mine and now I was doing the same, dipping when she led. "If you had told me before all this," she said that night, "about somebody with lung cancer and metastases in four places, I'd have said, 'Oh my God, he only has six months.' " Then she held out the slender, muscled arm with the IV and shook her head and smiled. "But these doctors don't know how strong I am."

All of this seems as though it were yesterday, or forever ago, in that crevasse between space and time that stays fixed in the imagination. I remember it all because I remember it all. In crisis with someone you love, the dialogue is as burnished as a scar on a tree. It shocks me now what I remember, though I suppose it shouldn't, because I have Caroline's voice fixed in my heart. That voice: the inflection, the range, the perfectly timed humor. This I would not lose.

By Monday, the effects of the chemotherapy had taken hold. Caroline had called her therapist—a man she had known and loved for two decades—in the first days of the diagnosis, but he had not yet been to the hospital; each of them may have been trying to postpone the grimness of the situation. That day she had lost whatever physical and psychological composure she possessed. She was violently ill, and weak, and I spent most of the afternoon sitting next to her while she slept. Four or five hours passed, during which Caroline would wake and start and then drift off again. I would exchange one cold rag for another and reassume my post. It was an odd and effortless station in which both time and thought disappeared. Later, Caroline told me she had dreamed all afternoon of me and her brother, who was in and out of the room as well.

When the phone rang I grabbed it to keep from waking her. "Caroline?" said a man's voice. "No," I said, "this is Gail." "Oh, Gail," her therapist said, recognizing my name and knowing his would be familiar to me. "This is David Herzog." I cupped my hand around the mouthpiece. "I was going to call you," I said. "You need to get up here. Now."

He was there that evening, and Caroline and I laughed later at my no-nonsense imperative—at my ability to do what she could not, which was to reach for him across the divide of fear. He was a bear of a man, and I became fiercely fond of him in the next few weeks, relying on his strength and straightforward kindness when the rest of the world seemed respondent to some deranged gyroscope. It was Herzog I spoke with when medical and emotional realities collided; he who called every day or two to see how I was holding up. I could talk openly with him about what Caroline was enduring and what time she had left. We assumed a ready-made mantle of intimacy that could not fail us: Ours was a wind tunnel attachment. We knew we were both central to Caroline's life, and we knew what we each stood to lose.

Here was another meadow of familiarity that Caroline and I had shared over the years. Herzog, as she called him, had been a pillar in the life she had rebuilt on the other side of anorexia. With our strong attachments to powerful fathers, we had each found sanctuary with male psychiatrists. More central was a mutual belief in psychodynamic therapy: the long, mountainous (often monotonous) version, in which you stayed in the room with your fears and history along with a witness who could bear the depths of your story. We lived in a cultural milieu—East Coast, post-1960s—in which therapy was taken for granted, and we each considered the work we'd done there crucial to who we were and to all ground gained. Caroline and I believed in the transformative power of therapy as surely as we did in AA or facing the truth or the loyalty of dogs.

Caroline stayed in the hospital for the rest of the week, until she was strong enough to go home; Morelli moved into her house to take care of her. The doctors wanted to get her stable with meds and radiation so that she might endure the next several weeks of chemotherapy. Her tribe of friends and extended family had taken on every detail of incapacitating illness; there were dog walkers and cooks and drivers at every changing of the guard. She had entered that zone of infirmity difficult for the worried well to appreciate: We were all circling her like heartbroken hens, while Caroline was simply trying to swallow a bagel or get through a phone call. At her insistence, she and I tried taking a short walk at Fresh

Pond with the dogs, maybe a hundred yards or so around the upper leg of the peninsula—a five-minute loop under normal circumstances that now took three times as long. We stopped on a bench to rest, gave the dogs a biscuit, started again. When she faltered, I put my arm out to steady her, a reversal of roles as wrenching as it was automatic.

She had started to exhibit small neurological symptoms, which I believe above all enraged her—she dropped a towel twice in front of me and refused to let me pick it up. We maintained a dialogue during these days that was partly code, but still as surefooted as Caroline used to be when crossing a stream. "You're just trying to get out of making me soup," I would say, referring to the old promise she'd made to cook for me when I got old. She called one night after she'd met with her oncologist for the first time outside the hospital, and started quoting the statistics on prognosis that were an optimistic version of what I'd read: the clinical trials under way, the new research studies at Mass General, the outside odds of two to five years to live. Her voice was soft and bright during this recitation, and I listened without saying anything, conscious of how harsh the light was in the living room.

"The point is to buy time," she said, and we were both dry-eyed and quiet. I didn't want her taking care of me and I wasn't sure how to take care of her, except to drive to chemo appointments and cook useless food and pay attention to her every cue.

But she broke down when she started losing her hair. "I know this seems ridiculous," she said. "But it's the only thing I can focus on. The rest is too huge." The man who had cut her long hair for years came over to her house that weekend to chop it all off; he brought a dozen roses and refused to take any money for his effort. I got a brochure on side effects and hair loss from the American Cancer Society and ordered a half dozen hats and scarves for her to wear, and one day in the waiting room outside chemotherapy we were looking through the catalog together and laughing, and tears started pouring down my face, even though I hadn't felt like crying. Now I couldn't stop. I shook my head and tried to dismiss her reaching for me.

"I'm afraid of letting you know how bad it is," I said. "I'm afraid if I tell you, you'll think I'm not strong enough to take it and you'll try to hide your fear."

"*Gail,*" she said. "I already know how bad it is. In some ways this is harder on you and Morelli than it is on me."

We were surrounded by other people waiting for chemo appointments, and no one even glanced our way during this exchange, except for one woman who passed us a box of tissues and went back to her magazine. I found this a relief and an education: No one in this place seemed uncomfortable at the emotions of strangers. We had entered a subterranean culture of extremis, where people were dying or trying to live and the heart was laid bare.

That was a bright afternoon at the beginning of May, and we had gotten to the hospital early and then sat outside in the sun, cross-legged on the ground and facing each other. By now Caroline's professional life had been put on hold, but she had one outstanding writing assignment she had forgotten to cancel, an essay about her and Lucille for a dog lovers' magazine.

"What am I supposed to write about?" she asked me. "That the only thing worse than losing your dog is knowing that you won't outlive her?"

Her voice was ragged, and I knew she was someplace past fear where I had never been, and I also knew that the best and hardest thing to do was keep my mouth shut and listen. Every false promise of hope or reassurance was a flight away from where we were now, which was sitting in the sun on the grass at Mount Auburn Hospital, my fingers circled around her wrists.

...

CAROLINE MARRIED MORELLI IN EARLY MAY, IN OUR friend Marjorie's backyard garden. If it was a wedding under fire, her friends turned it into something pastoral. The indomitable Sandy, Caroline's close friend and former editor at the *Phoenix*, was a tall redhead who now lived in Philadelphia. She burned up the highway during the weeks of Caroline's illness, arriving the week before the wedding with five pairs of red shoes for Caroline to choose from, and a vat of homemade rice pudding. Caroline's cousin Monique provided the knockout burgundy floor-length dress that she had been married in. The morning of the wedding, our friend Terry—who generally enlivened the neighborhood by keeping chickens in her backyard—lined the entire block leading to Marjorie's house with satin ribbons and lilies. Morelli did double duty as a photographer, a brilliant maneuver that gave him a way to get through the day while capturing it for the rest of us. Lucille was the ring bearer (Caroline had found her a satin pillow harness), and I her humble handler. Caroline had asked me to find a poem to read, one about love and commitment that was true to circumstance. I had searched for days for something appropriate: Most love poems don't assume storm clouds gathering overhead. But I understood what Caroline wanted; as much as she and I both longed for happy endings, we didn't necessarily believe in them. Now life was proving to be rougher than that in every dimension. I finally found a sonnet by Edna St. Vincent Millay that was both bearable and true, that spoke to Fate's destruction of "destiny's bright spinning." Caroline called while I was reading it.

"I have one," I said, "but I'm pretty sure it's too dark." Then I read her the first few lines. "I pray you if you love me, bear my joy / A little while, or let me weep your tears."

"That's it," she said abruptly, halfway through. "That's the one. You have to read it."

I have a photograph of the two of us that Morelli took that day: We are holding on to each other like a pair of saplings. The night after the wedding, she and Morelli and I were all flung on her sofa going over the details of the day. "How do you feel?" I said to Caroline, next to me on the couch, and she closed her eyes and smiled. "Consoled."

THREE DAYS LATER I flew to Austin for a four-day trip; I had been scheduled for months to appear at a university commencement. I called Caroline from my gate at the airport and made her laugh with a story about the security guards of a post-9/11 world, who had absconded briefly with my cowboy boots. Then my flight was called and my voice caught. "I don't want to leave you," I told her. "Go," she said. "Nothing is going to happen to me while you're gone." It was the last spoken conversation we would have. She called my home phone in Cambridge that night to leave a message, and said the doctors wanted her to come to the hospital the next day—they were worried about a couple of new neurological tics that they assumed were transient, a result of the radiation.

I had to be onstage for a two-hour ceremony at eight o'clock Friday morning; when I left the stage and checked my cell phone, I had three new messages. Caroline had been taken by ambulance to the emergency room in the middle of the night with what turned out to be a series of bleeds in the brain. She had lost the ability to speak; it wasn't yet clear what she could comprehend. I was standing on the University of Texas campus while I learned this, hearing it first from Caroline's cousin Suzanne, a physician, and then from Marjorie, who knew enough to tell me to come home. I found a flight routed through Chicago that left Austin that afternoon. I'd been given an honorary award that morning and, rushing to the car, I dropped the plaque I'd received on the street and chipped its frame. I almost left it lying there. It was an awful split second, as though all the little tokens of life were being swept away by the undertow of some darker truth. I got back to Cambridge after midnight.

Part of the abrupt horror of the next few days, for those of us who loved her, lay in not knowing precisely what had happened and what her experience of it was. Caroline's eyes were wild with fear when I walked into the hospital room. When someone told her I was there, she gave a cry of distress that meant two things to me. One was the simple voice of recognition. The other was that she knew what my presence meant, and how bad it must be if I had flown back across the country.

Take away the words and you find all the adornments that surround them. Body language, gestures, the story of the eyes. Morelli and Caroline's brother and sister were supposed to have full medical proxy, but the papers, drawn up that week, were not yet signed. We were trying to see if she could grasp the situation and hold a pen. I took her hand and said, "Caroline, it's me. If you can understand what I'm saying, squeeze my hand." She answered with an immediate, strong grip. "Okay," I said. "We need to get your signature on the proxy. If you think you can—" Her response interrupted me; she almost broke my hand. It was an entire sentence of meaning, full of impatience and efficiency. I held on to her while she scrawled her name on the forms.

Her arms became her eloquence from that day on. One night when I was sitting next to her bed, I laid my head down on the mattress beside her, and Morelli saw my weariness and got up to place a towel underneath my neck. It was one of countless acts of grace he provided in the next few weeks, when nothing much mattered but the light in the room and the number of breaths taken. Then Caroline flung out her arm and ran her hand through my hair, enough to comfort me for days, and we stayed that way until we both dropped into sleep.

We had spent years talking—talking when other people would have given up, teasing apart feelings and conversations and the intricacies of daily life. Now she couldn't talk anymore and so I didn't either; our narrative became a choreography of silence. I would spend hours at the end of her bed, not knowing much of the time if she even knew I was there. But Caroline and I had begun our friendship with a bond devoted to the elegant truths of nonverbal language: the physicality and hand signals and eye contact that dialogue with an animal entailed. When she had first fallen ill, I had brought to the hospital a T-shirt that she loved, from the Barking Dog Luncheonette in New York, with SIT! STAY! written on the back. I knew all about sit-stay, and how straightforward and essential it was, and so that was what I did. I sat and I stayed.

10

THAT GREAT HEART—OF COURSE IT TOOK HER A
long time to die. They had put in a central line of morphine within the first few days after the bleed, and so I
want to believe that her pain was contained enough by
the drug to let her float somewhere insouciant and free. I
cannot know this, any more than we can ever comprehend the next-door universe of the dying. But the question was what haunted me most, then and for months
after she was gone. I do know that suffering witnessed is
a cloudy and impotent world: The well, armed with consciousness, watch a scene they cannot really grasp or do
much to alter. Suffering is what changes the endgame,
changes death's mantle from black to white. It is a badly
lit corridor outside of time, a place of crushing weariness,
the only thing large enough to bully you into holding the
door for death.

Caroline lived for eighteen days from the night she
had the bleed. Morelli had all but moved into her hospi-

tal room, bringing Lucille with him. (One night, to our battle-worn delight, a new attendant walked out into the hall and said, with a grin on his face, "There's a goddamn dog in there!") I had an unnerving amount of energy during those weeks; I knew that grief was somewhere down the line and I staved it off as long as I could. I would take dinner to Morelli in the hospital, or talk to Herzog on the phone with my forehead in my hand. One afternoon I stayed on the phone for an hour with Louise in Minnesota while we both read poetry; the phone call was mostly silence, punctuated with "Aah!" and "Oh." I reached out in ways that were transient and intense, wept with no warning or not at all, was exceedingly polite to strangers. I called my friend Matthew from my cell phone while walking at Fresh Pond, and when I got his voice mail I left a long, rambling message with a halting question that seemed to me profound, a child's effort to understand the universe. "What if . . . ?" I cried. "I mean, I know this sounds stupid, but what if death . . . weren't a bad thing?"

However ingenuous the question, I know now that I was staggering toward the terrain of the other side of loss. Accepting a death sentence is like falling down a flight of stairs in slow motion. You take it in one bruise at a time—a blow, a landing, another short descent. I was on the verge of exhaustion, but I kept moving with a sense of frenzied purpose, as if I could outrun the fact of what was happening. I had found Herzog's home phone number the night after I got back from Texas, and called him that evening from the hospital. He came into the room carrying a handful of lilies of the valley—he knew that whatever else had happened, Caroline would be able to smell—and walked over to her and held them under her nose. It was a gesture that took my breath away with its exacting kindness, and in the next few weeks I spoke to him with a distress that I held in check around most everyone else who loved her. Near the end I asked him one night in the hospital corridor what he thought was happening, and he said, "Tell her everything you haven't said," and I smiled with relief. "There's nothing," I said. "I've already told her everything." The next day they took her off fluids, which was her wish, and when Morelli called to tell me it was done I let out a wail in my kitchen that was an animal's lament.

THE DETAILS OF dying are sad and grinding: breathing and waiting and breathing and waiting. The body, brilliant machine, knows how and when to close up shop. But Caroline was so strong, and so determined, that even in this final task she moved toward the end with bracing force. I had watched her on the water for years; now she was in the midst of what Anne Sexton had called "the awful rowing toward God."

And God, for me, was proving an elusive taskmaster. For most of my adult life I had been a lapsed Protestant or foxhole believer; I was always surprised by people who seemed certain about the answer in either direction. But my belief in something larger and more unknowable than human consciousness had never been held to the fire at such an intimate level. Sometimes I would go into the small hospital chapel and sit there in the dark, wearing its silence like a shawl, and then shrug and go back upstairs to Caroline's room. One especially bad night I remember staring at the light in the outside hallway and feeling the horrendous finality of this road—it seemed for that moment that the end was simply the end, like driving a car into a brick wall with nothing on the other side. It was one of the most desolate moments of my life, I think, and I felt as if the only God in the room that night was a morphine drip. And it came to me with cold comprehension that *this* was what it was to stare into nothing—a universe in which everything was pointless except the hardwired instinct to survive and endure and then die. What I was witnessing was as ordinary as morning, and now it was Caroline's time to fall, and I found the lack of light and meaning in that picture intolerable. No wonder we came up with the resurrection myth, I thought. It offered a crack in the blackness, the only way to tolerate this end.

Trying to recapture that bleary insight, I find that most of the power of it eludes me; we are wired to forget. We have to keep on: build bridges, learn language, have babies, beat a stick against a rock and find rhythm. When death shows up, the fragility of all this is revealed. But not for long. Remembering the suck and force of death is like trying to hold water in your hand. What I took away from that dark alleyway was that, when it came to God, I needed not to know—needed the humble ignorance as to whether anything existed outside that grim tableau. In the months that followed, I kept thinking of the phrase "requisite mystery," as though that could capture my necessary position in the universe now, poised on the line between Knowing and Not Knowing, between what seemed to me the arrogance of religious certainty and the despair of a godless world.

I MET A DEADLINE the day of the night she died. Not because I was acting tough, but because I knew she would die in the next twenty-four hours and that afterward I would collapse, and for now writing would buy me three or four hours in a relatively pain-free zone. I wrote that day because it was the only thing I knew to do, and I suspect it's what she would have wanted, and would have done herself.

I had been at the hospital until late the night before, a Sunday, and left her brother and sister and Morelli there and come back home and slept a frighteningly deep sleep for ten hours. Caroline had lost consciousness three days earlier. I had sat by her side counting breaths until the numbers themselves stopped making sense. When I last held on to her, she was burning up with fever and seemed to be working with furious energy, even in her stillness. She had left us all days before.

Monday night my phone rang a few minutes after midnight. I sat in bed staring at it while the machine picked up, and when I heard her brother's voice I thought for a split second, *If I don't pick up the phone she won't be dead.* Then I grabbed the phone and said, "Andrew?" and I heard his gentle voice telling me what I already knew. After we hung up I turned out the light and lay in the dark for a little while, and then I got up and called Sandy, Caroline's friend in Philadelphia, who answered on the first ring. We stayed on the phone for a long time, and we lit candles together at the same moment, like children capturing fireflies in a jar.

I stayed composed over the next few days in a way that alarmed me. Caroline knew concentric circles of people in and around Cambridge—dog people, writers, rowers, people in AA—and by now her illness was public enough that people often stopped me in the neighborhood to ask how she was. The afternoon after her death, I walked over to Fresh Pond with Clementine, and two or three people stopped me, and one older man broke down in tears when I told him. I had the unnerving calm of a chaplain. "I'm so sorry," I said, my hand on his arm. "She died last night at midnight."

I would learn to accept these periods of equanimity for what they were: reprieves from the vortex. But they startled me at the time, as did the foggy memory I would have of this later, along with a few other primal responses. I went home and started cooking enough black beans for an army, even though no one was scheduled to appear. I found myself counting friends with a child's cruel pragmatism—who was remaining in the tribe? When I realized I was doing this, with a singsong interior list-making, I scribbled down the names and posted them on the refrigerator: These were the people I could call at three a.m. I never called anyone at three a.m., probably because I had the list.

The black beans were gone by the end of the night. People started coming to my house and then kept coming, wandering through the kitchen into the backyard or sitting on the front steps. Marjorie, whose seasoned wisdom was born from her own losses, walked into my garden with a beautiful smile on her face; Tom called, crying—"Oh my God are you all right?"—then appeared with bags of Chinese food. Francesca, who didn't know Caroline but cared about me, walked in with a honeysuckle vine that's still growing in the tangle of the garden. Kathy, the dog trainer who had first connected us and had become a good friend, stood in the kitchen with her husband, Leo, crying and laughing while I told the story about Lake Chocorua and Caroline's mission to teach me how to row. There were dogs and people and empty plates all over the house until midnight, when I finally took an Ambien to sleep. Alongside all this heartache was an irony and a wonder. Caroline and I had reached out to each other from similar shelters of quiet and solitude. Now she was gone, and her leaving had flung open my doors in every direction.

The only education in grief that any of us ever gets is a crash course. Until Caroline died I had belonged to that other world, the place of innocence and linear expectations, where I thought grief was a simple, wrenching realm of sadness and longing that gradually receded. What that definition left out was the body blow that loss inflicts, as well as the temporary madness, and a range of less straightforward emotions shocking in their intensity. I would move as though I were underwater for weeks, maybe months, but those first few days between the death and the memorial service were a dazed cascade of tears and surprises. A part of me went through the appropriate motions with frightening alacrity: finding the poem to read at the chapel on Friday morning, practicing it aloud. But another part of me had the simple conviction that I wouldn't be able to get from point A to point B—that giving her over, in spirit and in public, was as perplexing and unfathomable as string theory. My old friend Pete, out of town when she died, called from Ohio to see how I was. I told him what I had been afraid to say. "I don't think I can do it," I said about getting through the service the next day. "I don't know *how* to do it."

He was quiet for a minute, and then he said something of such consolation that I will hear him saying it forever. "You know, Gail," he said, "we've been doing this as a species for a long time. And it's almost as if—it's like the body just knows what to do."

CAROLINE, WHO HALF BELIEVED that her circumspect existence kept her relatively unknown and thus protected from the masses, would have been amazed by the service. The chapel at Mount Auburn Cemetery was filled and overflowing. There was a cold, pelting rain all that morning, and Kathy had come to my house to get me; when we drove up to the entrance of the chapel I told her I didn't know if I could get inside. To her great credit, she did not rush to reassure me or assume I was speaking metaphorically. "Can you get to the door?" she asked. It was four yards away. So I got to the door, and Morelli was there waiting, and from there I was all right.

I read a poem that morning from Louise Bogan, "Song for the Last Act," the first lines of which are "Now that I have your face by heart, I look / Less at its features than its darkening frame." For two days after the service, I carried the meter of the poem in my head, a sweet interior background to the walks I took, the laps I swam, the last thoughts before sleep. It was as though some ancient choir had taken up residence inside me, giving me this exquisite chant, a measure of my own

movement and accompaniment to an otherwise un-
speakable sorrow. After two days, it disappeared as nat-
urally as rain on pavement.

...

THE RAVAGES OF EARLY GRIEF ARE SUCH A SHOCK:
wild, erratic, disconsolate. If only I could get to sorrow, I
thought, I could *do* sorrow. I wasn't ready for the sheer
physicality of it, the lead-lined overcoat of dull pain it
would take months to shake. Whatever I thought I knew
about loss—what I had anticipated about the After Caroline state, when the fear would be over, the worrying
ceased—I had no inkling that it would mean deliverance
into a new, immutable world. I lived in the reality of Caroline's absence all the time, it seems, and yet sometimes
the fact of it would nearly knock the wind out of me.
One night a couple of weeks after the service I tried to
make dinner for two friends, and I managed to get about
half a meal together before I realized I didn't know what
I was doing. They sat there kindly before their spartan
plates of chicken and rice—I had forgotten to make anything else—and I excused myself and went into the
kitchen and held on to the counter. She's *dead*, I thought.
The word itself was brutal. I had always disliked the eu-
phemisms the culture embraced for dying: "gone,"
"passed on," "passed away." They seemed avoidant and
sentimental, a way to bleach the concept of death of its

declarative force. Now I knew why we'd diluted the vo-
cabulary. *She's dead.*

I read everything I could to comprehend what I was
going through. *Mourning and Melancholia*, W. H. Auden,
Emily Dickinson. Poetry helped more than Freud. Pains-
takingly, probably automatically, I began separating the
Gordian knot of dual loss: My distress for Caroline in the
last weeks of her life was a different matter now from my
own battered loneliness. Everything about death is a cliché
until you're in it. I was half mad with desolation, and it
often came masked as anger. What the books don't tell you
is that some primitive rage can invade out of nowhere, the
only bearable alternative to being with the dead. Death is
a divorce nobody asked for; to live through it is to find a
way to disengage from what you thought you couldn't
stand to lose.

I found myself doubting or dismissing the intensity of
our friendship, as though I could discard the love and
therefore skip the pain. This worked for about twenty
minutes, or until I would say to someone we both knew,
"Oh well, maybe we weren't that close," and the listener
would burst out laughing. I started trying to remember
all the things I didn't like about her. There weren't very
many. Or I would take the boat out on the river and talk
to her aloud—so much and so often that I began to refer
to a certain stretch of water as the Church of Caroline. I
gave her reports on Lucille, told her about generous or
foolish things people had said or done, let her know how

all of us were holding up. One afternoon I had an inkling of how I must look—a solitary woman in a scull, smiling and talking to her invisible friend—and my chest seized with the potential nuttiness and emptiness of my one-way conversation. "What's worse?" I asked her. "If I talk to you and there's no one listening, or if you're there waiting and I *don't* talk to you?" I thought how helpless, probably irritated, she would feel at my silence. So I kept talking. I complained about incidents that had happened years before. "I don't think you should've been mad about my losing the boat seat," I would say. "It was an accident!" Or, "You were always in a hurry. Why were you in such a hurry?"

On a cloudy, windless day in late summer, Morelli and I met to move her boat from Riverside Boat Club, where Caroline had been a member for years, to my boat club a couple of miles upriver. It was a day we had both been anticipating, maybe fearing, for weeks, because we knew what Caroline looked like on the water and what rowing had meant to her. We parked my car at Cambridge Boat Club and drove together to Riverside, where a rower who had known Caroline helped us locate her scull and carry it from the inside bay down to the water. I had brought my own pair of oars; Morelli wanted to keep the set Caroline had used. No one spoke while we put in the boat and attached the oars. Then I hugged Morelli and they pushed me off from the dock, and Morelli stood there watching while I rowed away. Caroline had loved this boat and taught me to row in it; she had logged some five hundred miles a year for the last decade of her life. She had been a picture of stillness itself, carried by flight. I didn't want Morelli to see me break down, and for the first fifty yards I could concentrate only on this: that I had to keep going or he couldn't stand it. I got to the first bridge and made the turn, just beyond the last point where I knew he could see me. Then I squared the blades and pulled the boat into the shadows, and put my head on the grips and cried.

II.

MORELLI AND I TOOK CARE OF HER HOUSE ALL THROUGH the first winter, before it was sold, taking turns driving over to pick up mail or start the car or check on the heat. It was a particularly fierce winter, and I would walk into the foyer, where it was about fifty-five degrees, and feel the sadness ahead of me; it was like walking into fog. Life interrupted: Caroline's shoes were still lined up by the door; her coats—one for every kind of dog-walking weather—still had biscuits in the pockets. On her refrigerator door was a photograph of the two of us, our arms flung around each other, that Tom had taken that first summer at Chocorua. I could never bear to take the photo from where she had placed it years before, and one day when the house was being dismantled it simply disappeared—no doubt thrown out with the old spices and plastic bags and everything else that constitutes the bread crumb trail of a life. Morelli had taken Lucille to live with him since Caroline's last trip to the hospital, so her scent was gradually fading. I always made these trips to the house with Clementine, who barked with excitement and looked for Caroline and Lucille only on the first visit. Her nose must have told her what I could not, and after that she simply stayed by my side while I made my way through the house.

Some days I would sit in the cold living room and let the ache run free; it was the only place that I felt mirrored my heart. All my other places in the world—my own house, my connections with friends, my days with the dog or on the river or in the pool—were a refracted version of my grief; they all contained me, reflected the story, even helped me forget for a while. Here was the story itself. Here, in all its subcomfort temperatures and museum-like stillness, was Caroline, gone. It broke through my disbelief, my God bartering, my every other defense, and for this reason I both needed and hated to go there.

One afternoon when I had gone upstairs to check on things, I started going through her closet, the way we used to do together and like my sister and I had done when we were girls. I tried on sweaters and blouses that we had both loved, looking in the mirror while Clementine lay on the floor, watching me. "This looked better on you than it does on me," I would say to Caroline, and the dog would cock her head, and then I'd try on something else. I felt desperate while this was happening, and confused and guilty, and it has taken me years to remove myself enough from the pain of the incident to comprehend it. I wanted to claim whatever of her was left. I'd always heard stories about grief-stricken families arguing over ugly lamps or cheap coffeemakers; now I understood. The frantic hunger I felt was not trivial or greedy; it was possessive, in the most primal sense. I still have her gym bag and her rain jacket, and for a while I even tried to wear her winter boots, an entire size too big, which was absurd but comforting.

Memento mori: reminders of the dead. I think we must long for these signatures of history—the baseballs and ornaments and playing cards left on people's graves—because they take up the space left by the departed. The physical void after she was gone seemed alarmingly like a thing of physics, as if daylight had shifted or a house on the street had disappeared. Whenever Clementine heard the distinctive beep of a Toyota RAV, which is what Caroline had driven for years, she would wag her tail and start to head in that direction—pure conditioning that seemed to me a haiku of what was missing in the world.

YESTERDAY I FOUND a note I had written to myself, in the piles of outlines and narrative maps that are a writer's building blocks. "Let Her Die," I had written at the top of a legal pad, a shorthand reminder to get to that part of the story. Then I saw it the next day and half gasped; for a moment it was as though someone else had given me this instruction. Let her die: a three-word definition of the arc of grief if ever I heard one, and it takes a long time.

THE SUMMER AFTER I had learned to row, one evening on the river in 1998, I remember thinking that someday soon I would lose my beloved dad and that rowing and Caroline would help me through. We all count the tribe whenever we're scared. Modern Western society has mostly corralled this task within the realm of the nuclear family: The husband will clean out the garage or balance the accounts; the sister will be there to help after our folks are gone. But a huge portion of the world makes other allegiances, unconscious plans. Because of circumstance and desire, Caroline and I had each shifted a degree of that dependence onto each other—along with our siblings and Morelli, we were in line for the quotidian closeness, the emotional proximity of day-to-day life. Who has spare keys to the house, emergency contact numbers in the wallet? These are the lists you don't even consider before a certain age, when you're trying to get away from responsibility rather than acquire it. Then the list takes shape along with the attachments. Caroline and I had so thoroughly insinuated ourselves into this primary position that we joked about it for years, even after she reunited with Morelli. One afternoon weeks after she was gone, Morelli and Sandy and I were sitting on a park bench at the pond, talking with the combat candor of her three closest friends about how any of us could go on. "Oh God," I groaned, with mock distress. "Now I guess I'll have to get a boyfriend." Only the three of us, I think, would have found this so germane and so revealing.

LIFE'S IRREFUTABLE forward motion, a one-way arrow pointed past the dead. For months I felt the violence of time itself, as though some great barge carrying the rest of us had left Caroline stranded on the shore. I was raking leaves one day when I felt such a vast chasm of what was gone that I had to stop and sit down on the porch. All this raw material, from new shoots to compost in what seemed a single breath. Caroline was bone and ash and memory now, and I was raking dead leaves in the shelter of my garden while the bulbs, patient and thoughtless, waited to be planted. It seemed obscene.

"They take it all," I cried on the phone to Louise long-distance. "This husk of a life. And then you get to the end and you find out that death is godless, imminent, and cruel." Louise, who believed above all in the power of words, wrote this down while I was talking. And so she captured for me that moment none of us wants to remember, probably central to survival. *What if dying weren't a bad thing?* Caroline's death had left me with a great and terrible gift: how to live in a world where loss, some of it unbearable, is as common as dust or moonlight.

And then finally, unwittingly, acceptance wraps itself

around your heart. Late that year I was wandering through an open house in the neighborhood, and I saw a framed Pablo Neruda sonnet on the wall; it spoke to something spatial about loss that I had never before found articulated. Caroline's death was a vacancy in the heart, a place I neither could nor wished to fill. I had been confused by the prevalence of these feelings, the sense that her goneness was a thing unto itself, a memory outlined by crime tape it would be an outrage to remove. Now here was Neruda, entreating mourners to inhabit death as though it were a dwelling:

> *Absence is a house so vast*
> *that inside you will pass through its walls*
> *and hang pictures on the air.*

I LIVED IN THAT house of absence, took solace in it, until sorrow became a stand-in for what was gone. "Grief . . . remembers me of all his gracious parts," says Shakespeare's Constance in *King John,* about the loss of her son. "Then have I reason to be fond of grief." I knew I would never have another friend like Caroline; I suspected no one would ever know me so well again. That she was irreplaceable became a bittersweet loyalty: Her death was what I had now instead of her.

Grief is fundamentally a selfish business. Stripped of its elegant facade—the early onslaught of flowers and

casseroles and understanding—it is a place of such par-
ticularity that its arc is as complex as the relationship itself. People miss the warm presence in the bed, the laugh
in the evening, the gestures or countries or shared awareness traveled together. I missed Caroline in dozens of
ways, but through them all was the absence of the ongoing dialogue, real or imagined. "I miss *us*," she had said
that morning outside the hospital. For years, through the
trials of writing or dog training or life's ordinary bruises,
Caroline and I had been the soothing, modulated voice
in each other's heads. Now my thoughts were clanging
around unnoticed and unheard, lonely music with too
much bass. For months, I kept wanting to call her, half
assuming I could, to tell her what her dying had meant,
what her death had done to my life.

I DON'T KNOW MUCH of what I did that first year after
Caroline's death, beyond the usual rituals that were now
cloaked in a velvet silence. Walking, reading, watching
the light change. I sat on the couch in the living room
and read letters and cards from people who loved us
both, then reread them so that I could remember who we
were together. My friend Andrea dragged me to holiday
gatherings on the days I had usually spent with Caroline.
Rowing—God, I rowed until my hands were like leather
and my whole body ached with the fatigue my heart felt.
I would get back to the boathouse in evening light, pull

the boat out of the water, and wash and dry it as though I were hot-walking a horse. I know I wrote, though for months not much of it mattered. I puzzled, often and in private, over some promise of consciousness or design beyond the cold triumph of pure biology, muck and creation and reproduction and then muck again. Mostly I couldn't bear the indisputable lack of her, or the paltry notion that memory was all that eternal life really meant, and I spent too much time wondering where people got the fortitude or delusion to keep on moving past the static dead. Hope in the beginning feels like such a violation of the loss, and yet without it we couldn't survive. I had a friend who years before had lost her firstborn when he was an infant, and she told me one of the piercing consolations she received in her early grief was from a man who recognized the fierce loyalty one feels to the dead. "The real hell of this," he told her, "is that you're going to get through it." Like a starfish, the heart endures its amputation.

12

FOR YEARS I HAD TRIED TO PROTECT MYSELF FROM the psychic weight of New England winters by staying inside with tea and radiators, until I got a northern sled dog. Clementine took me out into the world in myriad ways, the most relentless of which had to do with the seasons. We walked through snowstorms and over icy trails; we walked in six p.m. darkness and single-digit temperatures. Because of her I had learned to love the light in winter—the rose gold of the sky an hour before dusk, framing the minimalist branches of the bare trees beneath. I fixed my routine to the light and to Clementine's desires. After Caroline was gone I vowed I would take the same walks, eventually finding solace in the missing space by my side.

So when I was through writing for the day, the dog and I would walk the few long blocks to the edge of Fresh Pond, an established oasis throughout the year, but populated in winter mostly by diehard joggers and dog walkers. Our usual path was a couple of miles round-trip; we would stroll through the woods to the deserted golf course, where Clemmie would chase geese to her heart's delight and bark at the exhaust signatures of planes across the sky.

One Friday afternoon at the end of January in 2004, I had driven over and parked by the soccer field on the edge of the reservoir almost a mile from my house; it was sixteen degrees outside, and I wanted to head straight for the woods. The days were growing longer and the light itself seemed brighter, and we walked for an hour under scudding clouds, nodding or saying hello to the other stalwarts who were on the path. Clementine was eight years old, at that point in a dog's life at which dignity and vitality are in step together, and she rarely strayed from my side, even off-lead in the woods. Whenever we left the reservoir, all I had to do was say, "Wait," and she would stop wherever she was, standing like a horse with her reins down while I attached her leash.

We had just come out of the woods onto the edge of the soccer field when I heard a man yell, "Get your dog!" Clemmie was next to me, unleashed, and we both stopped in our tracks, partly in response to the alarm in the man's voice. About ten yards away, by the bleachers, I saw a young muscle-bound man crouched on the ground, trying desperately to hold on to two pit bulls without collars or leashes. A second later the dogs broke free of his grip and came hurtling toward us. The larger dog, a gray-white male, knocked Clementine to the ground and grabbed her by the neck; the other dog went for her hindquarters. Clemmie weighed sixty pounds and had a full winter coat, which on a Samoyed is a three-inch-long double coat as dense as a carpet. She was thrashing and snapping at both dogs and I was screaming at the top of my lungs—"Get your goddamn dogs!"—while the man tried in vain to get ahold of the pit bulls.

I didn't yet know how badly Clemmie was hurt, or if the man was a tough guy or a fool, and there wasn't another soul around to help. The man finally got an arm around each dog's neck, and I grabbed Clementine's collar and cried out, "Please, just let us get to our car." The field was abutted by a chain-link fence, separating it from the street; I knew we had to get to that gate. He was struggling to maintain his hold on the dogs, and nodded, out of breath. *"Go!"* he called out. "I've got them." Clemmie was whimpering, panting to break free, and I held on to her and we started loping across the field.

We had made it halfway—about thirty yards—when I heard the man holler from behind, "Look out!" I felt the hair rise on the back of my neck. I turned around to see both dogs charging at a full run. Then I saw a flash of gray flying toward me through the air. The next thing I remember is being on my hands and knees on the ground. The gray missile was the larger male, who weighed about a hundred pounds; the female had gone after Clementine. When I scrambled to my feet, I saw

Clemmie on the ground a couple of yards away, with both dogs on top of her. One was at her throat and the other had its teeth on her belly. They had never made a sound.

My bladder emptied like a water balloon. I was wearing jeans, and realized with an almost serene detachment that they were drenched. I was in that state of adrenaline-soaked alacrity when the vision is sharp but tunneled and you feel you can do anything, and I felt not so much fear as a kind of wild horror. I had the flash that this must be what it was like to be in combat: The sympathetic nervous system mobilizes the body, which then gets rid of everything it doesn't need. Through no conscious effort of my own, I'd gone into automatic warrior mode.

I walked into the fight and started beating on the dogs' backs. Dressed for the frigid weather, I was wearing a heavy down jacket and fleece-lined mittens, and all the futility in that moment was captured by those mittens: I remember looking down while I flayed on the dogs and thinking that my hands looked like a child's. Then the female pit bull grabbed my forearm, almost casually, as if to move an obstacle away from its prey. The scariest part of this fleeting moment was not the violence the dog exhibited, but the control—my arm might as well have been a branch, for all the interest it held. You can generally gauge the seriousness of any dog attack by the noise and the restraint exhibited—the quieter it is, the more lethal the intent—and I had known from the start that this was a deadly situation. The pit bulls were after Clementine, not me. The female's hold on my arm gave Clementine the chance to wrestle away from the other dog, and she went tearing, at sled dog speed, into the woods.

By now the man had caught up to his dogs and was trying to get them under control. I went running after Clemmie, not knowing how severe her injuries were or where her panicked flight had taken her. I started calling her name and realized that my voice was nearly gone from yelling. It was after five p.m. and getting dark, and I was stumbling through snow in monochromatic woods. No one else was in sight. I remember thinking, with nonsensical logic, that I could probably search for her until about two a.m.—that I had that much time before I would need water or food, or before I would physically give out.

Years later, most of my visual memories of that afternoon have a cinematic purity—I remember what I was wearing, where I was standing, how my arms and face and voice felt while I scanned the blackening woods for a white dog. Micromoments have disappeared—I remember reaching my friend Peter's voice mail by cell phone, but I don't remember calling him or thinking to call him, only the sound of his recorded message. He lived four houses away from me and knew more about dogs than anyone I had ever known, and when I got his voice mail I coughed out something like "We were attacked by pit bulls and Clemmie is hurt and lost in the woods." He told me later that when he heard the message, he barely recognized my voice. Then I called Avery, who lived on the corner near the pond; she started heading in my direction. By the time she got to me ten minutes later, the first wave of adrenaline had passed and I had realized Clementine was lost, and I was shaking all over and finally terrified. Because my voice was gone, Avery kept calling out for Clemmie, and then my cell phone rang and I heard Peter, out of breath, say, "I'm running toward you."

In all the free falls of one's life, there are moments that stand out as a hand reaching across the abyss, and this, for me, was one of them. Without thinking I said, "No, go to my house first"—he lived down the street in the direction of the pond, which was separated from our houses by a major parkway. Two minutes later the phone rang again, so soon that I knew it had to be either good news or bad. Then I heard him cry, "I've got her!" and my knees went out from under me. Avery got me to my car and drove us to the house.

I've always wished for some witness to that day, someone who could come forward to tell me what Clementine's path had been. Once she broke away from the dogs, she had gone running into the woods alongside the reservoir, and she had had to cross a field beyond the woods and then a four-lane thoroughfare during evening rush hour. Then two more streets to the block where we lived, a trip of nearly a mile in city traffic. Peter had found her trembling on my front porch. She was bleeding and covered in pit bull saliva, and she had found her way home.

FOUR HOURS LATER, the vet and his assistant had shaved half of Clemmie's coat and begun closing the gaping wounds on her back and sides. Peter, whose father had been a horse trainer and who knew how to contain a thrashing animal, held on to Clemmie while they put her under anesthesia. The people in the veterinary practice had known me and my dog since she was a puppy, and Beth, my vet, had gone silent when I'd called to tell her about the attack; the two people left at the clinic had stayed late to wait for us when they found out what had happened. It was almost ten p.m. and none of us had eaten in hours, though I had remembered to grab a loaf of bread on my way out the door; I knew it was going to be a long night. After they got Clemmie under, I finally sank to the floor of the operating room with Cleo, Peter's Belgian shepherd, beside me. Clemmie was covered with puncture wounds on her hips and belly and violent gashes across her back; her thick double coat had probably saved her life. When they had finally closed the wounds and she began to emerge from the anesthesia, I crouched down by the operating table so she could see and smell me when she woke up. Maggie, who had been assisting the vet and holding Clementine while she was under, smiled at me across the table. "You know," she said, "you're doing a lot better than I thought you would be."

I was beaming. "Are you kidding?" I said. "She's *alive*."

IT WAS MORE THAN a week before Clementine could get beyond the driveway of my house without trembling, but as a sled dog, she had strong social instincts, and I think she recovered psychologically faster and better than I did. Besides being sore and exhausted, my only physical legacy from the attack was a black half-moon on my forearm I had found the next afternoon, a bruise the size of a pit bull's jaw where the female had grabbed me. The dog had bitten through a thick down coat and two sweaters to leave this mark, but I didn't feel or notice it until a day later, when the adrenaline had been replaced by a crushing fatigue. I fell apart on the phone to Louise, who loved dogs and loved me and knew how to care for both species in the worst of times. She sent white roses for the immediate pain and—ruthless acolyte to narrative—had an even better solution for the long-term damage. "I know this sounds cold," she said during our first conversation, "but are you taking notes?"

My intrepid Texas mother, who had just turned ninety, displayed a different brand of loyalty, more sword than pen and fierce enough to make me laugh with gratitude. She adored Clementine and was horrified by what had happened to both of us. "It just makes you want to pick up a gun, doesn't it?" she said on the phone one day when I was particularly shaken, and I answered, my voice trembling, "Yeah, it really does."

"Now, honey," she said, as though she were trying to placate a determined child, "you just can't."

THE PIT BULLS HAD been picked up by Animal Control and quarantined the day after the attack. Months of court appearances lay ahead, as well as a long campaign by the city to euthanize one dog and permanently sequester the other. For me there would also be flashbacks and fears and seemingly misplaced worries, the detritus of trauma that tends to insinuate itself into the psyche only after the danger has passed. I had already armed myself instinctively against some of this refuse with the simple power of narrative: From the moment I called Peter from the woods, the events of that day began shaping themselves into a bearable truth. And Caroline, who had long been the search-and-rescue spirit in my pantheon, was as essential as air to the retelling of the tale.

For about three weeks after the attack, I was certain that Caroline had saved Clementine that day—that she had gotten her away from the dogs and guided her through speeding traffic to safety. I believed this fully and categorically, with a sincerity that helped to shield me from the random iniquity of what had happened.

Clementine had achieved legendary status in the neighborhood within days after the assault, both for the horror of the story and for her odyssey home, and her wounds and shaved coat drew enough attention that strangers stopped to ask about us. When people who had known Caroline would see us at the pond, I would say, probably with the eyes of a madwoman, "I think Caroline saved her!" I was not known for such pronouncements, having a slant more empirical than mystical, and if people looked surprised when I told them this, they were kind enough to let me be. I had had a semiawake dream in the first few days after the attack in which I woke from a deep sleep and said to Caroline, in the dark of my room, "Oh my God—it was you, wasn't it?" And she responded with her soft, knowing laugh, amused by my slowness in recognizing the obvious. I wore my conviction like a Kryptonite shield for as long as I needed its powers, until I could stand in a field with the dog again without scanning the horizon for disaster.

And now? I doubt that I will ever be convinced in either direction. It is a story I still tell myself, framed within the magical thinking of a children's tale, where the forests are enchanted and the monsters vincible, where love and courage always trump danger.

"THE DEAD PROTECT US," I said to my friend Andrea at dinner one night when that bleak day in the field was behind me, long after I had stopped announcing that Caroline's spirit had shepherded us home. The words came out of my mouth with the certainty of litany, though I was only half sure of what I meant and unaware that I thought it until I spoke aloud. *The dead protect us.* I feel this now with an almost fierce relief. Caroline's dying had forced me into courage under fire; now I had her inside me as a silent sentinel. And whether one attributes this attachment to memory or to God, it is a consolation unlike any I have known. Thou art with me. "They take it all," I had cried on the phone to Louise that night, knocked down by despair. Turns out they don't take everything after all.

I LEARNED SOMETHING in the aftermath of the attack on Clementine that confused and alarmed me at the time. After so much fear and violence, here was my dog, safe and alive, and yet I worried about her with such maternal vengeance that it seemed to eclipse my grief for the dead. I was ashamed by the inconsolable quality of my anxiety; Clemmie was alive, and Caroline was gone, and yet my anguish now was about the one who had been saved. Then I realized something else they don't tell you in the instruction books for mourning: that we only fret about the living. I might well grieve Caroline for all my days, but I wasn't worried about her anymore.

Years after she was gone, I found the inscriptions

Caroline had written to me in two of her books—the first written a few months into our friendship, the second one two years later. We knew from the beginning, I think, that this friendship was different, that we would work to make it immune to the erosions of time. "For my dearest Gail," she had written at the beginning of *Pack of Two,* "with more love and gratitude than I have words to express. Your presence—in the world, in the woods, in this book—has altered the very texture of my life. Here's to all we have shared, and to many more years, many more miles with our beautiful girls."

Caroline's boat has rowed some two thousand miles since I moved it upriver on that calm day in 2002. I am fifteen years older now than Caroline would ever be; the rows are slower, but when I falter at the beginning of each season I close my eyes and visualize the precision of her stroke and straighten out my own. She is still my coach. One afternoon when I had come in from a five-mile row, as I was putting the boat into its bay, I said out loud to her, "You would be so proud of me." I meant because I had kept on rowing: Endurance was one of the traits we each admired in the other. But I know now that I meant something larger than the rowing, something that parallels the miles logged through fatigue and discouragement and inclement weather. Caroline would be so proud of me—proud of us—because I kept her, too.

13

CLEMENTINE WAS WITH ME FOR FOUR MORE YEARS. I used to lie next to her on the Persian rug in the dining room and wrap my arms around her and say, "Let's see if you can make it to thirteen. Can we do that?" And she would sigh her deep-chested sigh and roll over on her back. I had brought her home in 1995, when she was eight weeks old, on June 3, which was my father's eighty-first birthday. I thought at the time that after he died, I would have this dual anniversary to soften the sadness of the loss of him. Then Caroline died at midnight on the third of June, seven years later, and so the date had a wrenching significance.

That first year of raising a puppy, just before Caroline and I became friends, I had taken Clementine to Castle Island, a beach walk on Boston Harbor, on a windy day in March. We were walking across a long causeway when the wind picked up, and I saw her hesitate; she looked up at me for a directional cue, then plowed ahead. The first year or so with any dog is a steep relational curve—you are each finding out who the other is, and who you will be together. I knew at that moment, when we locked eyes and she started taking me forward, that we had become a team and that she knew it, too, and would go anywhere I asked.

In the ensuing decade, she had been integral to the most soul-stretching, joyful years of my life, and witness to some of the saddest. She led me into the woods with the closest woman friend I would ever have, and she was there waiting each night when I came home from the hospital where Caroline was dying. She was the sentry at the end of every trip I made back to Texas to care for my aging mother and father. After they were both gone, buried next to each other in the Texas sun, I flew back to Cambridge and Clementine nipped my nose when I walked in the front door, a gentle, herding nip, and then leaned against me and hardly left my side for days.

Old dogs can be a regal sight. Their exuberance settles over the years into a seasoned nobility, their routines become as locked into yours as the quietest and kindest of marriages. By the time she turned eleven, Clementine had started to lose her coat, a condition that can happen in older female Samoyeds, and so she was a far cry from the majestic white image of her earlier years. Once a model for the breed, now she looked like the velveteen rabbit, disheveled and patchy and loved into raggedness. Sometimes thoughtless people on the street would say,

"Ooh, what happened to your dog?" with more rubber-necking curiosity than genuine concern, and I would say, just to annoy them, "I think she looks a little like Katharine Hepburn; don't you?" She always looked the same to me. The last few years, our daily walks got slower and shorter. Sometimes we would make it only as far as the Virginia Woolf bench, a granite seat in the woods of Fresh Pond that overlooks the pond's edge and has on it an *Orlando* quote, and Clementine would lie under the bench while I lay upon it, watching the towering pine trees and the sky overhead. Or she would lie in the front yard next to me while I planted flowers, seeming content to survey the world rather than try to run it.

In spring of 2008, she started coughing with a bronchitis that wouldn't get better, and I knew we were in that passage of aged dogs where a constellation of symptoms presages the final outcome. I couldn't bear the idea that she might leave me on June 3, and that night I got down next to her on the floor and wrapped my arms around her and said, "Well, we made it, honey, didn't we?" Two nights later, she started going downhill fast. I got enough Valium in her to ease her distress, and when I walked into Angell Memorial Hospital at one-thirty in the morning, it was with the dry-mouthed certainty that I would be going home with her leash and collar but not with her. I had a close friend who was a veterinarian, who had known Clementine since she was a puppy, and she had insisted that I call her in the middle of the night when the time came. So Amy was there waiting for me in the hospital parking lot, ready to navigate the stark terrain of euthanasia and anonymous clinicians, and she was there on the floor beside us when we let her go. I was crying more than I wanted, afraid of upsetting Clementine, but she stayed calm, with her paw on my arm. "Go find Caroline," I said to her, and when she died she reached her front legs up toward me and rolled over into my arms, where I feel quite sure she will stay forever.

I DIDN'T WANT to leave her there. They tagged the body and we loaded her into Amy's van so that she could take her to be cremated in a couple of hours when the veterinary practice opened that morning. We sat in the van outside the hospital's bright, welcoming lights for a long time, talking and sometimes crying, Clementine's body in the back an odd comfort. I was staring into that too-familiar space of a world fresh with the initial disbelief of grief. It was nearly five a.m. when I walked back into my infernally quiet house, sadder than tears can ever tell, knowing that I was in the corridor of something far larger than I and that I just had to stand it and stay where I was. I went into the bedroom and saw the photograph of Caroline on my dresser, and I looked at her across that great divide and said, "Catch."

...

"CARLO DIED," EMILY DICKINSON WROTE HER FRIEND and mentor about the death of her beloved Newfoundland. "Would you instruct me now?" To say I could not bear this final departure is useless commentary, because bear I did and bear we do; to say I did not believe that I could is perhaps more to the point. Caroline and I had talked for years about the unthinkable notion of losing Lucille and Clementine; it seemed a graceful fluke of time that we would probably endure their deaths together.

Clementine's favorite denning spot in the backyard was under an enormous yew, a shrub so overgrown that a wild rosebush next to it has wound its way through and above the yew's branches. In spring, from the second-floor porch, it looks as if the yew has borne white blossoms— a magical hybrid of thorns and flowers and evergreens. Parlor tricks or God, I know now there are visions like this everywhere. Maybe this is the point: to embrace the core sadness of life without toppling headlong into it, or assuming it will define your days. The real trick is to let life, with all its ordinary missteps and regrets, be consistently more mysterious and alluring than its end.

Early in Clementine's life, when Caroline and I had forged the beginning depths of our bond, I took a house for a few weeks one summer in the woods of Truro on Cape Cod. Caroline and Lucille were meeting us there the next day. The evening I arrived, the caretakers in the large house on the grounds came by to tell me they were looking after the elderly woman inside—in her late nineties and failing day by day. I was not to be alarmed, they said, if I heard cars coming and going; they were on shifts of twenty-four-hour nursing care.

An hour later, at dusk, after I had unpacked the car with Clemmie by my side, one of the nurses came back and knocked on my door. "Mrs. C wondered if you could stop by," she said shyly. "She wants to see the big white dog." Clemmie had grown up around a neighbor in a wheelchair, so I wasn't concerned about her being gentle, and when we went inside the house, she walked over to Mrs. C's wheelchair and placed herself next to her hand. The woman's clouded eyes lit up, and she smiled as she ran her hand through Clementine's ruff. "I like a *big* dog," she said by way of introduction; she spoke with un-hesitant authority, as though we had just picked up a long-running conversation in which her opinion mat-tered greatly. However frail the rest of her was, all her strength was in her voice. "When I was growing up, I had Alsatians," she told me, her voice warm with memory. "They used to run through the woods here and terrify everyone." She smiled as she told me this story, and for a moment I could see her as a girl, fearless in the wilds of midcentury Truro, protected by her shepherd dogs and running free.

I've always thought there would be worse fates than to

be that woman, bowed but undaunted by everything physical in life, her memories and imperious presence outshining the waning light of aging. A woman still able to summon to her side a creature that nearly outweighed her; still able to say, with glad conviction, "I like a *big* dog." I like a big dog, too.

...

"THE HEART BREAKS *OPEN*," A FRIEND SAID TO ME upon Clementine's death. I know now that we never get over great losses; we absorb them, and they carve us into different, often kinder, creatures. Sometimes I think that the pain is what yields the solution. Grief and memory create their own narrative: This is the shining truth at the heart of Freud and Neruda and every war story ever told. The death mandates and gives rise to the story for the same reason that ancient tribes used to bury flowers with their dead. We tell the story to get them back, to capture the traces of footfalls through the snow.

After Caroline died, I made a list of things I wanted to accomplish before my life was over: write a book, go to Paris, find a great love, fit in as many dogs as I could. Oh, and find God, I said to a friend, the postscript that might change the world entire. Not a very long list, but everything on it seemed essential. I set out to achieve these things both systematically and unconsciously, aware that the map of one's life is made up of luck and circumstance and determination. I had always told Caroline that when I lost Clementine, I planned to go to Paris, cry my heart out for six months, then come home and get a puppy.

Paris is still on the list. The spring of Clemmie's decline was exhausting and heartbreaking, and I was no more fit to travel abroad when she was gone than I was to bike to the moon. Instead I spent the summer in the shadows of sorrow and anxiety, wondering how I would navigate the world without her in it. The very fact of me felt diminished.

I laid the flowers people brought me on her denning spot by the yew, and when they had yellowed I piled more on top, so that there was a pallet of dried flowers where she had lain. I sat on the porch and talked to her, as I had talked to Caroline after she was gone and to Clemmie throughout her life. I found out from listening to memory and silence that I didn't much care, at least then, about going to Paris. That what I wanted was the breath in the house and the warmth and demands of someone who needed me. "It's *your* love," my old friend Pete had said to me years before, when I was trying to leave a lousy relationship. "You get to keep that." My love: precious, lonely gift.

I spent an hour one afternoon on the phone with a breeder of Border collies, a stranger who understood my distress and stayed in touch with me for months afterward, toward no other end than kindness. Peter, who had helped save Clementine that cold day years before, knew what I had lost but couldn't express it, so most days, after he and Shiloh, his young Belgian shepherd, had had their run, he would open my back door and holler, "Dog!" In she would come, my auxiliary shepherd for the morning, who had long since added me to her pack and who probably sensed Clemmie's departure before she was gone. Shiloh would lie down beside me for an hour while I wrote, as focused and calm as a visiting nurse.

THE OLD NAVAJO WEAVERS used to insert an unmatched thread into each of their rugs, a contrasting color that runs to the outside edge. You can spot an authentic rug by this intentional flaw, which is called a spirit line, meant to release the energy trapped inside the rug and pave the way for the next creation.

Every story in life worth holding on to has to have a spirit line. You can call this hope or tomorrow or the "and then" of narrative itself, but without it—without that bright, dissonant fact of the unknown, of what we cannot control—consciousness and everything with it would tumble inward and implode. The universe insists that what is fixed is also finite.

ON A BRIGHT, HOT day at the end of summer, I got on a plane not to Paris but to Baltimore, on a mission more circuitous and less glamorous than a trip to the Louvre. I rented a car at the Baltimore airport and started driving from Maryland across rural Pennsylvania, on my way to meet a breeder of Samoyeds whose dogs I had seen a decade before. That part of the state has a rustic, southern feel, full of back roads and green, rolling hills, with barn stars on half the houses. I had been up since dawn and was alone and half lost, wondering what in the hell I was doing on a lonely stretch of Pennsylvania when I might have been in Italy, say, or Montana, or the south of France. I passed a small highway marker, as discreet as a street sign, that read MASON DIXON LINE, and my heart fluttered in response.

Just beyond the marker, on the other side of the road, was a seedy-looking liquor store with a purple neon sign. I traveled a lot when I was a drinker—alcohol gave me the high-octane courage to go anywhere—and wherever I landed, the first thing I did, had to do, was find the nearest liquor store. I always pretended it was a mission of desire, but it felt like a prison sentence. When I drove past the store in Pennsylvania, its parking lot half full of cars in the early afternoon, I had a flash of what it had been like to have to do that, to locate the place that warehoused my bottle of hope.

But the store with its flashing light—LIQUOR—also reminded me of something else from years before that nearly made me laugh aloud. When I was growing up in Texas, whenever a fellow was going to the liquor store or stepping out to the car to have a snort, the colloquial expression was "I've got to see a man about a dog." Now here I was, so many miles and decades later, sober and heartsore and still alive, and I really did have to see someone about a dog. She was part of a litter that had been born in June, and though I hadn't laid eyes on her, I had already named her: Tula, a wonderful old southern name I'd always loved. I had searched out the name's origins and loved it even more. Tula was from the Sanskrit for "balance," or from "tulayati," meaning "to lift up."

The clouds ran on ahead of me and I crossed into Gettysburg, a place of such sacred ground and memory that it threw my own life into the panoramic mist where it belonged. I drove into the military park and onto the old battlegrounds, and I stopped at the cemetery long enough to pay my respects. Then I got back in the car and kept on going.

ACKNOWLEDGMENTS

MY EDITOR, KATE MEDINA, UNDERSTOOD THE VISION
of this book from its conception; my thanks are on every
page. Louise Erdrich, darkling sister, was invaluable as
both writer and friend. My agent, Lane Zachary, offered
her usual blend of enthusiasm and Buddhist calm. Andrea Cohen, poet and jokester, reminded me always of
the seriousness of humor.

The emotional staying power I needed to tell this
story came from many sources. For their grace and kindness, within the story itself and to me afterward, my
great thanks and love to Mark Morelli, Sandra Shea, Re-
becca Knapp, and David Herzog.

My home fires were tended by an exceptional group
of friends: Peter and Pat Wright, Kathy and Leo De
Natale, Avery Rimer, Rick Weissbourd, Peter James,
Marjorie Gatchell, Eliza Gagnon, Louisa Williams,
and the Saturday night gang. Amy Kantor and Beth

Shepherd took care of me in every way. I know it would make Caroline happy that this list is so long and full. Finally, my love and gratitude to Dick Chasin, who knew the depth of my grief as well as the journey through it.

LET'S TAKE THE
LONG WAY HOME

Gail Caldwell

A Reader's Guide

Kelly Corrigan is the author of two *New York Times* best-selling memoirs, *The Middle Place* and *Lift*. She is a You-Tube sensation whose beloved "Transcending" video was sent woman-to-woman to more than four million viewers. She is also a contributor to *O: The Oprah Magazine* and *Glamour* and is the founder of circusofcancer.org and Notes & Words (a performance series combining authors and musicians). She lives outside San Francisco with her husband and children.

Kelly Corrigan: I cried a lot reading this book, thinking about people I couldn't stand to lose, my necessary pillars, as you say. I can imagine how much it hurt to write and rewrite it and then open the bound manuscript for the first time and not be able to hand it to Caroline. But I also know this book keeps her alive in some ways, keeps her name in conversation. How has all this—writing, publishing, reading—affected your grieving?

Gail Caldwell: The jury's still out on this one. I've finally accepted after all these years, having lost both my father and mother, that grief itself is a lifelong process. That's not really bad news. Loss reshapes you, and I think if you can bear staying inside it for a time, there are great blessings on the other side of all that sorrow.

I do know one palpable victory that all this has given me: a record, if you will, of Caroline and me that lives outside of my own shifting interiors. I can look at the book or read from it, or hear readers respond to it, and think, "Well, there we are." It's a great consolation.

KC: I'm a big fan of fighting—if that's what it takes to keep a relationship real. There's nothing more depressing to me than falseness and niceties and the unspoken. I think you feel the same way, and I think this is exactly what distinguished your friendship with Caroline. Is that right?

GC: There were so many things, in retrospect, that distinguished our friendship that they've all blurred together into one mosaic: humor, intensity, shared loves. I do think that each of us had a commitment to emotional honesty in relationships that matter, and we acknowledged early on that this one mattered to us, and that we would do what was necessary to keep it real, keep it free of the baggage of the unspoken, as you put it. Probably the fallout of years of therapy on both our parts. Not everyone wants to "communicate" this way, but we were evenly matched. It might have driven some people crazy, but in our case I think it was liberating—it helped to establish and maintain the trust between us.

KC: I think it's hard to find something new to say about love and friendship. Your first line all but acknowledges that you agree. How anxious were you about crossing the line between familiar and trite?

GC: That wasn't really a concern for me. Eudora Welty once said that there are something like seven stories in the world, and that we just keep retelling them. I was less worried about saying something new than I was about saying something real. I think that the truth, or success, of any writer's story lies partly in its specificity and its emotional honesty. I wanted to deliver the depth of the connection I had with Caroline, as well as the loss of her, and convey those things to the reader without sentimentality.

When I wrote that first line that you mention—"It's an old, old story: I had a friend and we shared everything, and then she died and so we shared that, too"—it was all I could write of the book for a year. I left it lying on a legal pad until I was able to go back and begin to tell the story. It seemed to me then, as now, that the oldest stories are sometimes the simplest and the most universal.

KC: I was so knocked out by your observations—not wanting to throw out your friend's spare keys, for example. Was it hard for you to revisit those moments?

GC: The most meaningful passages for me were also, not surprisingly, the most difficult, or at least bittersweet, to write. I love the memory of us in the woods together, and the sound of Caroline's voice, and how funny she was. The wrenching parts, from after she got sick—they belong to another country.

One thing I realized as soon as I began the book was that all the memories, good and bad, seem to have been there waiting for me to unearth and articulate. That's the beauty of the unconscious, and the heart's archive: nothing ever really goes away.

KC: I don't have a dog. And I never did. What am I missing?

GC: Oh, good, now I get to quote Caroline, from *Pack of Two*: "wildness and nurturance and trust and joy." I'm writing about dogs in my next book, and I spend huge swatches of time watching and thinking about what they give us and evoke from us. Clementine, my first Samoyed, had such grace and equanimity that I used to refer to her as my better half.

Living in the company of another species (particularly Samoyeds, who are great clowns) teaches me enormous things: humility, patience, love, the mystery of connection, much of it nonverbal. Plus you get to play in the snow, walk in the woods, continually make a fool of yourself. And you have a built-in social excuse: "Sorry, I have to walk the dog."

KC: I know from my own experiences that illness is humbling. It's hard to need so much help, even for the most comfortable among us. Those who suffer from alcoholism need a lot of help. Do you think your personal histories with alcohol informed the way you cared for Caroline and the way she responded?

GC: I never thought about our shared history as having this effect, but I'm sure there's some truth to it, at least from my end. Illness is the great equalizer, isn't it? You can't go through something as searing as facing alcoholism, which brought each of us to our knees, without some sense of having broken open that last private space of autonomy and trust. In AA they call it the gift of desperation, because you're forced to let people in.

My caring for Caroline, to the small degree that I was able, was unthinking and automatic. But her illness and its trajectory were so brutally swift that we were doing everything on the run. I think it was probably easier for Caroline to worry about me than about herself; certainly I know the reverse was true.

KC: Over the course of a year, because of the topics of my own books, I end up talking an unnatural amount about dying and crisis. I wonder sometimes if I am becoming less sensitive—like a doctor who has lost her bedside manner. Have any calluses grown where you used to be tender?

GC: Maybe I'm a little tougher. Not harder, but hardier. At readings and signings, I've been moved and astonished by the commonality of this experience, and by what readers have been willing to share with me. It's a universal language.

I hope I understand other people's losses a little better, and don't feel the need to rush in and fix things. I love Annie Proulx's line on this: "If you can't fix it you've got to stand it."

1. Caldwell writes, "Finding Caroline was like placing a personal ad for an imaginary friend, then having her show up at your door funnier and better than you had conceived." She goes on to describe their fantasy of a "tatting center," and the secret codes that tied their lives together. To what degree do you think the strength of a friendship depends on being able to disappear into an imaginary world together, to develop a secret code that only the friends understand? How do you see this playing out in *Let's Take the Long Way Home*? What about in your own life?

2. Gail and Caroline have a great deal in common, but they also have very different personalities. There is a darker edge to their friendship, too; what Caldwell calls the swampland of "envy and rivalry and self-doubt" that can exist between women. They met their competitive-

ness head-on, in writing, on the water, and in life. Do you think this emotional honesty strengthened their friendship? In what ways are they similar, and in what ways different? Do you think these elements strengthen or weaken their bond?

3. Both Gail and Caroline have relationships with men, and yet the core of their friendship seems to contain a singular intimacy that exists between women. Does that bond call to mind friendships or relationships in your own life?

4. In a scene on the Harvard University sports fields, Caldwell says, "We used to laugh that people with common sense or without dogs were somewhere in a warm restaurant, or traveling, or otherwise living the sort of life that all of us think, from time to time, that we ought to be living or at least desiring." One of the things Gail and Caroline discuss in the course of their friendship is whether they are "living [their] lives correctly"— whether they are taking full advantage of the time they have. Do you think there is a "correct" way to live, and if so, what do you think should dictate the priorities? Is it realistic to try to avoid wasting time, or is that necessary to "correct living"? Do you think *Let's Take the Long Way Home* offers any kind of answer to this question?

5. "What they never tell you about grief is that missing someone is the simple part." What do you think Caldwell means by this?

6. In what ways does Clementine's arrival change Gail's life, on both a practical and an emotional level? She compares dog ownership to having children, but makes the point that "this mysterious, intelligent animal I had brought into my life seemed to me not a stand-in, but a blessing."

7. As the author is struggling to overcome her alcoholism, she has two conversations that help change the way she sees the world, and her experiences. In one, a therapist tells her that "If . . . I could keep only *one thing* about you, it would be your too-muchness." And her alcoholism counselor, Rich, says, "Don't you *know*? The flaw is the thing we love." Do you agree? Can you think of examples, in the book or in your own life, that prove or disprove these ideas?

8. *Let's Take the Long Way Home* doesn't have a memoir's traditional chronological narrative structure. How do you think this contributes to the effect and emotional impact of the book overall? Does it reflect the nature of the friendship itself? Could Caldwell have told her story any other way?

9. Do you see Gail, as a character, change in the course of the book—having discovered, and then lost, both Caroline and Clementine? What would you say she has gained?

10. Caldwell tells a moving anecdote about using the "alpha roll" while she is training Clementine. It is a technique meant to establish the dog owner's authority, but it doesn't work at all on the mischievous puppy; as she continues to try and fail, Caldwell suddenly sees a parallel to her own childhood relationship with her father and senses that the whole approach is wrong. "From that moment on, everything changed between us. Wherever I danced, she followed." What lessons might we all learn from this story?

11. Loss is at the center of the book—we know from the first several pages that Caroline will die—and Caldwell writes about the new world without Caroline in it, where she experienced rage and despair and "the violence of time itself." Does her description of grief mirror any of your own experiences?

12. Caroline and Gail have a private game in which they assign a dog breed to each person they know. For fun, what kind of dog would you be? What about your best friend? Your worst enemy?

GAIL CALDWELL was awarded the Pulitzer Prize for Distinguished Criticism in 2001. She is the former chief book critic of *The Boston Globe* and the author of *A Strong West Wind; Let's Take the Long Way Home;* and *New Life, No Instructions.* She lives in Cambridge, Massachusetts.

Look for Gail Caldwell's

A STRONG WEST WIND

"Moving and magical . . .
[a] great American memoir." —*Elle*

In this exquisitely rendered memoir set on the high
plains of Texas, Gail Caldwell transforms into art what
it is like to come of age in a particular time and place.

A Strong West Wind is a memoir of culture and
history—of fathers and daughters, of two world wars
and the passionate rebellions of the sixties. But it is also
about the mythology of place and the evolution of a
sensibility: about how literature can shape and
even anticipate a life.

Random House Trade Paperbacks